Workshop Models for Family Life Education

Adult Survivors of Child Sexual Abuse

Christine A. Courtois

Families International, Inc.
Milwaukee, Wisconsin

Illustrated on the cover is an oil painting by artist Jane Orleman of Ellensburg, Washington, called *Sunk in Gloom*. Since 1990, Ms. Orleman, a survivor of childhood physical and sexual abuse, has painted more than 180 pictures dealing with her childhood experiences and their aftermath.

Copyright 1993
Families International, Inc.
Published in association with
Family Service America, Inc.
11700 West Lake Park Drive
Milwaukee, Wisconsin 53224

Library of Congress Cataloging-in-Publication Data

Courtois, Christine A.
     Adult survivors of child sexual abuse / Christine A. Courtois.
        p. cm. — (Workshop models for family life education)
     Includes bibliographical references.
     ISBN 0-87304-247-6
     1. Adult child sexual abuse victims—Psychology. 2. Adult child
sexual abuse victims—Rehabilitation. 3. Group psychotherapy.
     I. Title.   II. Series.
     HV6570.C68 1993
     362.7'6—dc20   93-18434

CONTENTS

PREFACE

Workshop Models for Family Life Education is a series of manuals intended to promote the exploration of new alternatives and the utilization of new options in day-to-day living through programs in family life education.

Basically, family life education (FLE) is a service of planned intervention that applies the dynamic process of group learning to improving the quality of individual and family living. The manuals are in workshop format and offer new approaches to service to families. They are meant to serve as a training mechanism and basic framework for group leaders involved in FLE workshops.

In 1974, the Family Service Association of America (FSAA), now Family Service America, Inc., appointed a National Task Force on Family Life Education, Development, and Enrichment. One of the goals of the task force was to assess the importance and future direction of FLE services within family service agencies. One of the recommendations of its report was to "recognize family life education, development, and enrichment as one of the three major services of the family service agency: family counseling, family life education, and family advocacy."[1] This recommendation was adopted by the association's board of directors and has become basic policy.

An interest in FLE is a natural development of Family Service America's role in the strengthening of family life and complementary to the more traditional remedial functions of family agencies. Family life education programs can add a new dimension to the services provided by family agencies. They can open an agency to the general population by providing programs that are appropriate for all families and individuals, not only for those at risk. They provide a new arena for service that deals with growth as well as dysfunction. They can encourage agencies to look beyond the therapeutic approach and to take on a new objective for the enrichment and strengthening of family life. For the participants, FLE programs can lead to increased understanding of normal stress, growth of esteem for one's self and others, development of communications skills, improved ability to cope with problem situations, development of problem-solving skills, and maximization of family and individual potential.

This series provides tangible evidence of Family Service America's continuing interest in FLE and of a belief in its future importance for family services. Family life education programs, coordinated within a total agency program and viewed as a vital and integral part of the agency, can become key factors in promoting growth and development within all families.

NOTE

1. "Overview of Findings of the FSAA Task Force on Family Life Education, Development, and Enrichment," mimeographed (New York: Family Service Association of America, May 1976), p. 21.

ACKNOWLEDGMENTS

I am most grateful to a number of people for their assistance in producing this workbook. I thank Ralph Burant, editor of the Workshop Models for Family Life Education series, for his encouragement. Thanks also go to David Drum for his careful review of the manuscript and many helpful suggestions and to Jane Gilbert and Gretchen Boules for their field testing of this workshop model and evaluative comments. Special thanks go to Constance Robinson, who gently nudged me to keep on track and patiently typed and retyped the manuscript. I also would like to acknowledge the support and intellectual stimulation I derived from my weekly consultation groups, both in my private practice and in local community mental health centers; members of the staff of the Center for Abuse Recovery & Empowerment at the Psychiatric Institute of Washington; and to all the adult survivors with whom we work. Last, but not least, I thank Tom for all of his support.

Christine A. Courtois

INTRODUCTION

This workshop grew out of my experience over the past 15 years as a researcher and therapist working with adult survivors of child sexual abuse. I have led numerous therapy groups for this population and recognized the need for a structured, short-term group workshop with an informational focus such as the one presented here.

It has become widely recognized in recent years that survivors of child sexual abuse continue to be affected into adulthood and regularly seek therapy for their symptoms. In fact, they make up a disproportionate percentage of individuals who use mental health services. Until recently, victims/survivors have had little or no opportunity either to get information about sexual abuse or to share their experiences with others. Abuse was kept hidden and not discussed; the silence contributed to feelings of confusion and shame in the child, which often persisted into adulthood. The goal of this workshop is to provide participants with a wealth of information about abuse, how it occurs, and its aftereffects. The hope is that this information will help the participant feel better about him- or herself (or about someone known to have been sexually abused) and resolve associated feelings.

Child sexual abuse that occurs in families (between relatives or between people who function in family roles) is referred to as *incest*. Sexual abuse that occurs outside the family is referred to as *sexual abuse* or *molestation*. Significant problems within the family contribute to incestuous sexual abuse. Incest often has extensive repercussions because of the betrayal that occurs when the abuser is a relative or someone in a close relationship to the child.

Child sexual abuse as a result of living within a dysfunctional family system causes numerous life concerns for both child victims and adult survivors, including difficulty trusting others; with feelings or the expression of feelings, especially anger; with intimate and parenting relationships; with shame and low self-esteem; with depression and panic reactions; with feelings of numbness and emptiness inside; with psychosomatic illnesses, including headaches and gastrointestinal problems; with self-damaging behaviors or thoughts; with chemical dependency and other addictive and compulsive behaviors, including eating disorders; with time loss, memory gaps, and sense of unreality; with flashbacks, intrusive thoughts, and images; with sleep disturbance (sleepwalking, nightmares, and insomnia). Tendencies toward codependence and workaholism are also evident in this population.

The objectives of this workshop for adult survivors of child sexual abuse are to provide a structured, supportive group experience of 8 to 10 sessions (depending upon the leaders' and group members' preference) in which individuals are able to gain information about child sexual abuse and its current and later effects on their life. Furthermore, the workshop is designed to help participants become aware of the connection between past experiences of abuse and present functioning. The workshop explores in considerable detail what constitutes sexual abuse; what the sexually abused child experiences at the time of abuse and later; the rules, roles, and dysfunctions in the family in which incest occurs; issues specific to adults molested as children; and the importance of healing, remembering, and discussing the abuse within a self-help or therapy environment.

A primary goal of the workshop is to lessen the isolation and the sense of being different or contaminated that adult survivors so often report and to encourage participants to examine and reverse the rules and roles of the family within which the abuse occurred. The goals of solidarity and sharing with others are achieved through the identification of commonalities as individuals relate their experiences and feelings to one another. This is facilitated by the group leaders, who strive to create an atmosphere of encouragement, acknowledgment, and validation. The mini-lectures are designed to help group members achieve a cognitive understanding of what happened to them or to someone they know as well as how it happened. The group exercises are designed to deepen their understanding and to help elicit emotional reactions.

GENERAL INFORMATION

This time-limited, structured workshop comprises 8 to 10 two-hour sessions. It is recommended that membership be limited to between 8 and 12 participants. A smaller group provides more psychological safety for individuals with a history of child sexual abuse; the small size allows more time to share and engage in group discussion and fewer people with whom to interact.

Mini-lectures are presented to provide concrete information about child sexual abuse to the group members. Individual and group exercises, as well as the full-group discussions, provide opportunities to experience and share emotions. The lectures and exercises are carefully sequenced to help participants sort through the information they receive and deal with the emotions that are evoked by the material.

The workshop design promotes balance between intellectual understanding and emotional awareness. Although emotional expression is encouraged, it must be handled with sensitivity and tact on the part of the group leaders. The workshop is *not* intended to provide therapy or group treatment, but rather to be a stimulus to understanding child sexual abuse and its dynamics, its emotional aftermath, and other consequences. The process of recovery from the aftereffects of abuse is also emphasized. This psychoeducational model is deliberate in design; the workshop's structure is intended to increase the participants' sense of security to allow safe exploration of their past life and present functioning.[1]

Two leaders per group are recommended due to the intensity of the material covered and the reactions that might be stimulated. One leader can monitor participant reactions while the other presents didactic information. Leaders can trade roles during the course of the workshop. Together, leaders should model mutual respect, cooperation, and problem solving (which may contrast markedly from participants' experience in their families and thus provide an *in vivo* model for change).

Group leaders must have extensive knowledge about child sexual abuse and the familial and societal dynamics that support it, along with knowledge of many of the issues reported by adult survivors. The leaders must be knowledgeable enough to answer factual questions related to child sexual abuse and must be attuned to emotional consequences and nuances in order to validate participants' feelings. They must also be straightforward in acknowledging what they do not know and be willing to find answers to questions that can't be answered on the spot.

To gain mastery of the material, group leaders should read extensively on child sexual abuse and its aftereffects. Recommended reading includes *The Courage to Heal* (1988) by Ellen Bass and Laura Davis; *I Never Told Anyone: Writing by Women Survivors of Child Sexual Abuse* (1983) by Ellen Bass and Linda Thornton; *Secret Survivors: Uncovering Incest and Its Aftereffects in*

Women (1990) by E. Sue Blume; *Allies in Healing* (1991) by Laura Davis; *Outgrowing the Pain* (1984) by Eliana Gil; *Toxic Parents: Overcoming Their Hurtful Legacy and Reclaiming Your Life* (1989) by Susan Forward; *The Other Side of the Family* (1990) by Ellen Ratner; and *Healing the Incest Wound: Adult Survivors in Therapy* (1988) by Christine Courtois. Books are also available on the sexual abuse of boys—*Abused Boys: The Neglected Victims of Sexual Abuse* (1990) by Mic Hunter and *Victims No Longer: Men Recovering from Incest and Other Child Sexual Abuse* (1988) by Mike Lew.

Workbooks that might be useful to participants include *The Courage to Heal Workbook* (1990) by Laura Davis; *Incest, Years After; Learning to Cope Successfully* (1987) by Mary Ann Donaldson and Susan Green; *Growing beyond Abuse; A Workbook for Survivors of Sexual Exploitation or Childhood Sexual Abuse* (1990) by Signe Nestingen and Laurel Lewis; and *The Woman Inside: A Resource Guide to Lead Women from Incest Victim to Survivor* (1989) by Patty Barnes.

Leaders must research applicable legal statutes in their state regarding reporting disclosures of past or ongoing sexual abuse. It is likely that participants will discuss their own past abuse or that of other family members or friends; however, they might also disclose their own continuing abuse or the current abuse of someone else. Many states require mental health professionals to report disclosures of ongoing abuse when the names of the victim, the abuser, or both are known. Privileged communication is suspended when active abuse is reported.

Leaders must be well-prepared and knowledgeable about the content of each session. They must be familiar with the entire workshop manual and should review and prepare for each session before presenting it. Main lecture material should not be presented in standard lecture format; rather, the leaders should strive to present material in a warm and informal manner so as to encourage questions and responses. Eye contact and a comfortable, inviting style help put participants at ease with this difficult topic.

The leaders who do best are those who have had previous experience leading short-term psychoeducational and/or structured groups and therefore have a basic understanding of this type of group. Leaders need skill in group management, in that their role is that of facilitator–observer monitoring participants' reactions throughout the course of the group. Leaders may have to break the ice on difficult subjects, reinforce responses, and clarify and interpret material. Books on group process with adult abuse survivors are available: *Grown-Up Abused Children* (1985) by James Leehan and Laura Wilson; *Group Psychotherapy with Adult Children of Alcoholics: Treatment Techniques and Countertransference Considerations* (1989) by Marsha Vanicelli; and *Adult Children of Alcoholics* (1988) by Phyllis Tainey. Finally, books and articles on post-traumatic therapy such as *Trauma and Its Wake* (vol. 1 and 2, 1985, 1986), edited by Charles Figley, and *Post-Traumatic Therapy and Victims of Violence* (1988), edited by Frank Ochberg.

Leaders should arrange chairs in a circle or semicircle and list exercise questions on a flip chart or blackboard before participants arrive. To the extent possible, the leaders should create a comfortable and pleasing setting in which to run the group. A flip chart or chalkboard is an important teaching tool to help members visualize the material presented. Written or displayed material is an effective way of highlighting and reinforcing the information being communicated.

The content of this workshop has been carefully sequenced; each session builds upon the material of the previous session. For the sake of continuity, sessions are presented in sequence; a lot of material is covered each week. Participants should be advised of this fact before beginning the group and at the beginning of each session. As members begin to feel at ease with the workshop and its content, discussion will increase and leaders may find it difficult to cover the session content as outlined. Leaders should draw the points of the mini-lecture from the discussion in order to highlight them and focus on information from the discussion that has not been touched upon in the mini-lectures. If it is necessary or useful to do so, the workshop can be extended to 10 or even 12 sessions to allow more time for group discussion as well as help group members identify with one another.

In some groups, members will engage one another rather spontaneously. In others, it will take longer for members to feel comfortable. Whether the group develops slowly or quickly, discussion is likely to increase and intensify over the course of the workshop. Members can be expected to experience and discuss painful feelings and memories: sadness, grief, guilt, confusion, anger, shame, and fear. Leaders must be prepared for a full range of emotional reactions and strive to respond empathetically to whatever is expressed. In this manner, feelings are encouraged while empathy and compassion are modeled. Individual follow-up, including referral for therapy, may be needed after a particularly intense group session or if a group member's reactions become troublesome between sessions. It would be useful for leaders to develop a list of local treatment and self-help resources ahead of time.

Group leaders should feel free to modify the curriculum for this workshop according to the needs of the group or their own personal style. Even though the model is highly structured, its primary goal is the dissemination of information to the participants and the promotion of active discussion.[2]

PREPARATION FOR THE WORKSHOP

Recruiting

Successful recruiting usually involves combining several different approaches. Group leaders who are associated with schools or who practice privately, at a community mental health center, a family service agency, a hospital, a business, or any other setting can begin by recruiting within the agency and from among his or her own clients. Other professionals are often good referral sources and should be made aware of the group, including its objectives, structure, and duration. Many therapists search for a group such as this one for their adult survivor clients and clients' concerned friends or relatives. Clients themselves should be recruited by providing information about the benefits of the group experience and how its design is geared to meet specific needs. Flyers announcing the availability of the group and newspaper articles are useful recruiting techniques. Public service radio and TV announcements also generate inquiries from interested individuals. For example,

> It is estimated that approximately one in three girls and one in four boys have been sexually abused as children, either by someone they knew or by a stranger. Because sexual abuse was a hidden problem, a child most often did not disclose the abuse or receive appropriate assistance. As a result, adult survivors of child sexual abuse often feel isolated from others and have difficulty with trust, intimacy, and communication. They also may suffer from shame and low self-worth, depression and anxiety, fear of abandonment and rejection, problems with relationships, substance abuse, eating disorders, and difficulty with anger. Such problems lend themselves to support from others and discussion in a group format.

> If you or someone you know has had these experiences and is concerned about these issues, [name of organization or agency] is sponsoring a workshop for you called "Adult Survivors of Child

Sexual Abuse." The workshop is educational in focus and involves discussion with other group members. For more information or to register, call [agency phone number], that's [repeat number]. Registration for each workshop is limited to 12 members.

Newspapers can be approached to run a special article on the workshop or on child sexual abuse and its aftereffects or to announce the starting date of a new program in their community events listing.

Registration

General screening and registration can be done over the telephone, although some leaders prefer to meet potential group members in person. When interested individuals call for information, they should be told that the workshop is not a therapy group or a self-help program, but rather an adult education workshop with an emphasis on information and personal reactions to abuse. Prospective clients should be given an overview of the workshop, the title and content of each session, and information about dates, time, location, and fee. The group leaders, their qualifications, and their commitment to the group should also be discussed during the telephone call.

Participants need not have had a personal experience of child sexual abuse in order to join; however, survivors are encouraged to register. The leaders will most likely encounter ambivalence on the part of some prospective members who are former victims. On the one hand, these individuals are often reluctant to discuss their sexual abuse experience. On the other hand, they may long for the opportunity to do so. Some individuals may be hesitant to register for the workshop and others may express hesitation about sharing anything about themselves or their experience. Prospective members should be told that they must make a commitment to attend all sessions and that their feelings of reluctance are understandable and shared by other members of the group (whether abuse survivors or not).

Prospective members should also be advised that they are in control of what and how much they choose to reveal. They will not be pressured to discuss more than is comfortable for them. They should, however, be told to anticipate the use of exercises and that they will be encouraged to explore their own feelings and to interact with other participants. Members should also be told that confidentiality is discussed in the first session of the group. It is suggested that group members arrive 15–20 minutes before the first meeting so that they can register, pay the workshop fee, and complete any additional paperwork. Name tags should be used for the first few sessions so that members can learn one another's names, which facilitates discussion. It is also beneficial to have a handout with the dates and topics of all sessions.

In addition to a written schedule, the leaders might want to provide a handout listing group guidelines, especially concerning privacy and confidentiality. Establishing a group routine helps provide continuity and familiarity from session to session. This includes a brief check-in time (or group go-round) with everyone at the beginning of each session, followed by discussion of any administrative matters, leftover issues from the previous session(s), review of the day's session, mini-lectures, exercises, discussions, and closing.

The meeting room should be of adequate size to hold a circle (or semicircle) of participants. The room needs to be relatively comfortable, private, and free from outside interference and distractions. The room also ought to be large enough for group members to break into dyads or small groups and to comfortably engage in discussions. Chairs should be placed in an open circle with the leaders sitting opposite each other and with one of them near the flip chart or chalkboard.

NOTES

1. Group leaders must be aware of reporting laws in their state regarding the disclosure of past or current sexual abuse. This information should be conveyed to all prospective members and discussed with the entire group during the first session for clarity and informed consent.

2. In field testing this model, some leaders have found it useful to extend the workshop by two sessions, one after Session 4 and one after Session 7, in order to allow more processing and discussion time and to finish any incomplete exercises.

SESSION 1
BACKGROUND INFORMATION ON CHILD SEXUAL ABUSE

OBJECTIVES

✔ To provide information on the prevalence of child sexual abuse and incest

✔ To define child sexual abuse and incest and to discuss different types and categories of abuse

✔ To examine the incest taboo and how it has extended to other forms of child sexual abuse

✔ To discuss how sexual abuse occurs

I. INTRODUCTION

A. *Welcome and Handouts.* As members enter the room, provide them with a name tag, the workshop outline (handout 1), group guidelines (handout 2), and bibliography (handout 3) and welcome them individually. Handout 1 can be posted on newsprint in the room, where it should remain for the duration of the group.

B. *Leader Introductions.* When all group members are present, the leaders should again welcome them, then introduce themselves to the group by name, position and/or title, and any other appropriate identifying information. The leaders may share some information about their professional or personal backgrounds to facilitate group comfort and confidence.

C. *Introduction of Group Members.* Ask participants to move about the room in order to introduce themselves briefly to other members. Instruct the group as follows:

As a way of "breaking the ice" and getting to know one another, we would like to spend the next 10 minutes walking around the room. Briefly introduce yourself to each person in the room, including the leaders. When you meet someone new, say at least one thing about yourself that you did not mention previously to another participant.

The group reconvenes after introductions are completed. Group discussion should be encouraged before continuing with the introduction of the workshop.

D. *Purpose of Workshop.* Leaders can begin by discussing the purpose of the group:

You are here because you are interested in learning more about how child sexual abuse affects children and how it continues to affect adults. You may be here because you or someone close to you was sexually abused as a child and you are now interested in learning more about the effects of such abuse. You may also be interested in learning about how and why children are sexually abused, what sexual abuse is, and how to prevent its occurrence. The group's purpose is to provide information about sexual abuse and its patterns of occurrence, to discuss the concerns that can develop from being sexually abused as a child, and to increase awareness of how these childhood problems can continue to affect one's adult life.

There are two types of child sexual abuse, depending on who is involved. Within a family context and between individuals related by blood, marriage, family relationships, or familiarity, it is known as *incest.* Incest is distinguished from *molestation,* which occurs between strangers or distant acquaintances. Participants in this workshop will learn about these two main forms of child sexual abuse.

It is believed that as many as one in three girls and one in four to seven boys have been sexually abused. Girls are more likely to be abused *within the family* by a relative; boys are more likely to be abused *outside the family* by a stranger or acquaintance. (Of course, some boys are abused by family members and some girls by strangers.) Some are abused both by relatives or acquaintances and also by strangers. Unfortunately, it is not unusual for some children to be abused over time by several different individuals. The first experience of abuse may make them at risk for further abuse.

Sexual abuse can be touch or nontouch. It ranges from relatively mild forms, such as observation, nudity, kissing, or fondling, to more serious forms, such as oral sex or intercourse. (Note: Abuse usually escalates over time, and its form does not always determine the intensity of the victim's response. Abuse of a "milder" sort may have serious aftereffects.) Sexual abuse, especially incest, often goes on for years. Force and violence are sometimes used to threaten the child into compliance. Other means of involving the child include threats, trickery, or blackmail.

The term *victim* refers to the child victim of sexual abuse; *victim survivor, adult survivor,* and *adult child* refer to adults who experienced such abuse as children. Child victims and adult survivors show a wide variety of aftereffects from their abuse experience. All victim survivors respond individually according to who they are, how the abuse occurred (for how long, how often, how old they were when it began and ended, what sexual behavior was involved, who was involved, whether it was disclosed or discovered, whether anyone helped or stopped it), how their family functioned, other life experiences they had, and whether they had positive relationships with others, both inside and outside the family.

When sexual abuse occurs within the family (incest), the family often attempts to deny its occurrence and keep it a secret from relatives as well as outsiders. Secrecy is the result of shame and loyalty among family members. Unfortunately, secrecy results in more

19

stress for the child, who is often blamed for the activity and discouraged from reporting it and thus "embarrassing" the family. When sexual abuse occurs outside the family, the family is more likely to respond in a way that assists and protects the child. The family is not so caught in a web of divided loyalty and humiliation when the abuser is not kin.

To recover from the effects of child sexual abuse, many survivors benefit from individual and group therapy and involvement in self-help groups. Some survivors are able to recover within the context of good adult relationships, but almost all need education and therapy to assist them in working through their feelings of shame and isolation. Through therapy and education, survivors learn that sexual abuse did not happen only to them and that they have much in common with other victim survivors. They give and receive caring and assistance as they share the secrets of their childhood abuse with others who have had similar experiences.

This group is not a treatment or therapy group; however, it provides some therapeutic benefits for participants. Resources are provided during the course of the workshop for those who may need or want to seek further treatment from professionals and regarding other recovery options as well.

E. *Overview of Format and Content.* This workshop is a structured, time-limited group that meets for eight or more sessions. Meetings are two hours long and begin promptly. If you cannot attend a session, please let the leader know ahead of time, if possible. Each of you has committed to attending all sessions, barring illness, crisis, or major scheduling conflict.

Mini-lectures are used to provide you with information on the topic of sexual abuse. Throughout most of the workshop, we will ask you to work in pairs and small groups before holding full-group discussions so that you can share more easily and draw on your personal experiences. *Please share only as much as you feel comfortable sharing. You do not have to disclose any more than you want.* There is no pressure for you to disclose or discuss more than you feel ready or able to discuss. However, in our experience, we have found that members who share tend to get the most out of the group. Some of these topics are painful and difficult to discuss, especially if you have not previously spoken about them or if they are extremely embarrassing or shameful to you. As you learn more about sexual abuse, it will likely become easier for you to accept yourself and your feelings and to share them with others.

A lot of material is covered in these sessions. At times, you may feel overwhelmed and not have enough time to discuss or absorb the information. Because of the amount of material to be covered, it is sometimes necessary to move on to the next topic without discussing a topic as completely or as thoroughly as you or we would like. Please let the leaders know if too much material is being presented too quickly, if you are having uncomfortable reactions, or if you'd like additional sessions or suggestions for follow-up reading or support.

Please note that *confidentiality is an important issue. Personal material discussed in group is private and must stay in the group.* It is necessary for all members to respect the confidentiality of other members and not identify them by name or membership outside the group setting. Members must pay special attention to issues of confidentiality to increase the sense of safety and security associated with group participation. Open sharing and discussion will not occur in a setting that is not perceived to be safe. Thus, at this time, each of us vows to maintain the confidentiality of this group.

Do you have any questions or comments at this time?

II. EXERCISE ONE: SHARING MEMBERS' EXPECTATIONS OF THE GROUP

A. Objective: To provide members with an opportunity to express what they would like to learn from the group.

B. Assign members to triads.

C. Request that they share with their partners what they hope to get from the group and why they joined.

D. Debrief: Members return to the large group to discuss their reasons for joining the workshop and their expectations of it.

E. Leaders list responses on the flip chart. This list of expectations is used for review at the end of the group.

F. Leaders ask if there are any questions or need for further discussion.

III. MINI-LECTURE: WHY WE SHOULD LEARN ABOUT CHILD SEXUAL ABUSE AND INCEST

A. The following information is drawn from the sources listed in the references for this session.

1. The bulk of child sexual abuse is perpetrated either by a family member or someone known to the child.
2. Females are more likely to be sexually abused within the family and males are more likely to be abused outside the family, although males do experience family sexual abuse and females are abused by strangers and acquaintances.
3. A very high percentage of the female population (possibly 40% or higher) has had an experience of sexual abuse at some time during childhood. Possibly one in four males has been so abused.
4. The majority of abusers of both male and female victims are male; however, some unknown percentage of abusers are female. Abuse by males is usually more overt; abuse by females is more likely to be covert and therefore more difficult to identify. Abuse by a female may also be more difficult for others to believe and to understand and thus causes the victim additional shame.
5. The most common pattern of sexual abuse begins with non-threatening, mild (and possibly pleasurable) attention and sexu-

al contact. It may, but does not always, involve touch. Observation, exhibitionistic nudity, and showing a child pornography are nontouch forms of sexual abuse. Over time, the sexual activity is repeated, usually progressing to more serious forms. For example, it may go from observation to fondling to oral sex to intercourse.

6. The average age of the child when abuse begins is between 8 and 12, but for many children it begins at a much younger age, sometimes even in infancy and when the child is preverbal. Abuse that occurs at a very young age and is forceful and repeated is the most likely to be forgotten or repressed by the child.

7. The average duration of abuse within the family is four years. Abuse that occurs outside the family is usually of shorter duration because the abuser has less opportunity for contact with the child.

8. Most sexual abuse does not involve force, but it does involve some sort of manipulation and misrepresentation to the child. Even when abuse is nonforceful, it is violating and therefore a form of violence. Children are taught to obey adults. Adults can use their authority to influence the child, including coercing them into participating in sexual activity or contact. Children may also be frightened into participation by an abuser who threatens harm, abandonment, rejection, and so forth. In some cases, physical force, violence, or threats and coercion are used.

9. Children are dependent upon adults and are not yet mature— other reasons they might be easily influenced or manipulated. Children are also quite accessible or available to adults, especially to family members and friends or acquaintances.

10. The abuser almost always tries to get the child to keep the secret by scaring and threatening him or her into silence. Even when the abuser says nothing is wrong with the sexual contact, the secrecy often makes the child feel that it is bad and wrong. Many children internalize these feelings and end up feeling bad, dirty, and as though something is wrong with them.

11. Some reactions to sexual abuse are mild and some are very severe. Each child reacts in an individual way. Many of these reactions continue into adulthood, whereas some begin in adult-

hood after years of delay. These reactions, too, range from mild to severe.

12. Child victims, especially when no help is available and the abuse continues and escalates, are at risk for many negative feelings and reactions.

13. Child victims and adult survivors often have very low self-esteem, are unable to trust others, need to be in control and feel safe, and deny feelings and needs. Because they were betrayed and used by people who should have protected them, they end up fearing and mistrusting others. Often, they feel vulnerable instead of comfortable when they get too close to others. Relationships may be fraught with difficulty, and intimacy and parenting may be especially threatening. Survivors commonly feel isolated and different from others and may attempt to gain approval by taking care of others or by being excessively dependent. Some may cope with their fears by being controlling of themselves or others or by being extremely rigid.

14. Child sexual abuse often results in emotional problems. A number of studies have found that approximately 40% to 50% of people who seek mental health services have been sexually abused as children. Psychological problems associated with molestation include chronic depression, anxiety and phobias, guilt and shame, physical problems, emotional numbness, eating disorders, self-mutilation and suicide attempts, revictimizations such as battering relationships and rape, and addictions, compulsions, and codependence. These "second order" problems disrupt adult lives and cause adults to seek mental health care. It is necessary to see these problems not as pathology but as adaptations that have later developed into life difficulties.

B. The lives of children who have been sexually abused are altered, sometimes dramatically. Much of their psychological energy may be tied up in coping with the abuse. Child victims lose their innocence at an early age and learn that abuse is the price of love. With incest, they lose their sense of the good and protective parent and safe family. They feel isolated from others as well as different and marked.

They wonder what is wrong with them and why no one sees, listens, believes, or helps them. *They end up feeling it must be their fault or the result of something about them.* Some abusers even tell them it's because they are bad or deserve abuse. *No child deserves abuse, no matter what an abuser says.*

The child usually learns to keep the abuse secret and not to tell anyone for fear of being blamed or hurt, to protect others, or even to please the abuser. Sexual abuse, especially incest, was formerly considered a taboo subject: it was believed to be exceptionally rare or a fantasy that was not to be discussed in civilized company. This prohibition left the abused child isolated, forced to cope as best he or she could under the circumstances. As a result, *many children learned to deny their own feelings and reality because no one believed them and they received no assistance.* They often become very good at hiding themselves and concealing their real feelings and needs in order to protect themselves and the secret. In many instances, they lose memory of some or all of the abuse, especially if it occurred forcefully and repeatedly when they were very young.

Unfortunately, sexual abuse flourishes in silence and secrecy, leaving the child with little or no recourse. It is only since the early 1980s that sexual abuse has been exposed and discussed openly. It has been acknowledged as a social problem with grave consequences for the individual, families, and society at large. It often spawns further abuse as well as numerous disruptive aftereffects. With disclosure of the problem, help is now available to heal the effects of abuse.

IV. EXERCISE TWO: HOW DO I FEEL LEARNING ABOUT AND TALKING ABOUT SEXUAL ABUSE?

A. Objective: To provide members with the opportunity to express their reactions and feelings in response to the information in the mini-lecture.

B. Ask members to pair up with someone new (not the same person in the first exercise and not someone whom they know).

C. Suggest that they discuss with their partner their reactions to the mini-lecture. They might also share whether they have ever openly discussed sexual abuse (in general or their own) and why or why not? How does it feel to do so?

D. Debrief: Members gather to discuss these same questions with the larger group.

E. Leaders list responses on the flip chart.

F. Leaders close the group at this time by asking participants whether they have questions, concerns, or reactions to today's group discussion. Leaders should encourage a closing discussion and summarize themes arising in the session (e.g., confusion, shame, anger, outrage) and commonalities among members. These items are written on the flip chart or chalkboard and saved for future sessions. Participants are thanked for joining and for their participation.

G. The leaders should let members know they may have some residual reactions between sessions to each week's content. Feelings such as anxiety, fear, relief, and outrage are normal and expected. If a member's feelings become overly strong or uncomfortable between sessions, the group member should seek support from friends or relatives or call the leaders. The leaders should also state that some members may not want to return for the next session as a result of their reactions. Participants are reminded that they have committed themselves to attending the entire workshop and that they will be supported in coping with their fears and other emotions. Discussing abuse and its effects is often difficult but marks the beginning of new self-understanding and self-acceptance.

V. BACKGROUND MATERIAL FOR GROUP LEADERS

Most abused children adapt to the abuse as best they can in isolation and without assistance. When abuse occurs in the family, it is generally repeated and escalates in severity; as a result, the repercussions of incest are often more serious than those of molestation. Additionally, sexual abuse perpetrated by a family member makes disclosure and intervention efforts more difficult because of family bonds and divided loyalty. The child's story is open to challenge and disbelief. When the child's word is pitted against an adult's, many adults find it easier to believe the adult. As a result, incestuously abused children develop coping mechanisms to deal with the abuse, which is often ongoing, its consequences, and their inability to stop it or gain effective intervention or protection.

Incest usually occurs within the context of other family problems. Frequently, the parents' marriage or intimate relationship is riddled with power imbalances, communication difficulties, and sexual problems. The relationship may also be characterized by bouts of violence. One or both parents may be alcoholic or otherwise chemically dependent. The parents may have little to offer their children and, in fact, may use their children for their own needs. Children raised in these circumstances essentially parent themselves. They experience neglect and unpredictability. Behavior that one day brings praise and reward, another day brings neglect and abuse. The sudden shifts in the parents' mood and attention confuse the child and usually cause feelings of insecurity, anxiety, attachment, and dependence.

When sexual abuse occurs in a family situation such as this, the child hopes for but does not expect to receive assistance. Rather, the child believes that disclosure will bring blame or criticism rather than effective assistance. The child may not be believed by other family members, who wish to maintain loyalty to the abusive relative and keep the family together. Such behaviors further confuse the child and reinforce his or her sense of badness and worthlessness. The child feels that he or she deserves the abuse and does not deserve help. Consequently, the child is unable to develop trust and, later in life, has problems with closeness and intimacy. The child grows up not knowing what to expect from others and does not have the familial security, attachment, or consistency necessary for his or her full personal development.

When sexual abuse is ongoing and progressive, trauma is exacerbated. The child develops strong defenses in order to cope, which in turn deflects psychological energy away from the tasks of normal development.

Secrecy, silence, and taboos keep the child from asking for help and from getting acknowledgment and validation of the experience. In effect, *the child's sense of reality is negated*, leaving him or her to wonder what is real and what is not. The child often wonders what he or she did that was so bad to deserve being abused and not being assisted.

At the time of the abuse, children develop symptoms associated with post-traumatic stress disorder. These symptoms frequently go untreated as the abuse goes unattended. Although some of these effects may heal over time, usually under the influence of good, trustworthy relationships, some become chronic or are delayed, causing "second level" problems to develop. The most common effects include chronic depression and anxiety reactions, self-destructive and self-defeating behaviors, eating disorders, substance abuse, sexual difficulties, dissociative disorders, somatization disorders, explosive and aggressive behavior, and revictimization in other relationships, both within and outside the family setting. These secondary problems, in turn, create new problems and are usually what cause the adult survivor to experience distress and to seek mental health assistance.

BIBLIOGRAPHY

Blume, E. S. (1990). *Secret survivors*. New York: John Wiley.

Courtois, C. A. (1988). *Healing the incest wound: Adult survivors in therapy*. New York: W. W. Norton.

Finkelhor, D. (1986). *A sourcebook on child sexual abuse*. Beverly Hills, CA: Sage Publications.

Russell, D. E. H. (1986). *The secret trauma: Incest in the lives of girls and women*. New York: Basic Books.

Summit, R. (1983). The child sexual abuse accommodation syndrome. *Child Abuse and Neglect, 7*, 177–193.

HANDOUT 1

WORKSHOP OUTLINE

This group has been developed for adolescents and adults who were sexually abused in childhood or who know someone who was abused. The purpose of the group is to increase the awareness of these individuals about what constitutes child sexual abuse and incest and about reactions of adult survivors. The purpose of the group is not to diagnose or provide treatment, but rather to provide education to foster increased awareness. Resources are provided for treatment and support on an as-needed basis.

SESSION 1: BACKGROUND INFORMATION ON CHILD SEXUAL ABUSE

✔ Introduction
✔ Exercise One: Sharing Members' Expectations of the Group
✔ Mini-lecture: Why We Should Learn about Child Sexual Abuse and Incest
✔ Exercise Two: How Do I Feel Learning about and Talking about Sexual Abuse?

SESSION 2: THE CONTEXT OF SEXUAL ABUSE: FAMILY RULES AND DYSFUNCTION

✔ Opening the Session
✔ Mini-lecture: The Family—From Functional to Dysfunctional
✔ Exercise One: How Family Dysfunction Can Contribute to Sexual Abuse Both inside and outside the Family and How Healthy Family Functioning Works against Abuse
✔ Mini-lecture: How Dysfunction Contributes to Sexual Abuse inside and outside the Family
✔ Mini-lecture: Common Rules and Negative Messages in Dysfunctional Families

✔ Exercise Two: How Family Rules and Messages Support Sexual Abuse

✔ Mini-lecture: How Rigid Family Rules and Negative Messages Support Sexual Abuse within and outside the Family

SESSION 3: CHILD SEXUAL ABUSE AS TRAUMA

✔ Opening the Session

✔ Mini-lecture: What Is Trauma and What Are Post-Traumatic Stress Reactions?

✔ Exercise One: Characteristics of Post-Traumatic Stress Reactions

✔ Mini-lecture: What Makes Sexual Abuse or Incest Traumatic for the Child?

✔ Exercise Two: Discussion of Sexual Abuse/Incest Factors

✔ Mini-lecture: Factors Related to Secondary Stress Reactions; Protective Factors That Moderate or Modulate the Trauma

✔ Exercise Three: Factors Related to Secondary Stress Reactions

SESSION 4: COMMON EFFECTS OF CHILD SEXUAL ABUSE

✔ Opening the Session

✔ Mini-lecture: Initial Effects of Child Sexual Abuse

✔ Exercise One: Participants' Awareness of Initial Effects of Child   Sexual Abuse

✔ Mini-lecture: Long-Term Effects of Child Sexual Abuse

✔ Exercise Two: Participants' Awareness of Long-Term Effects of Child Sexual Abuse

✔ Exercise Three: Recognizing Strengths and Developing Perspective

SESSION 5: COPING WITH THE AFTERMATH OF SEXUAL ABUSE TRAUMA IN CHILDHOOD AND ADULTHOOD

✔ Opening the Session
✔ Exercise One: Children's Feelings after Being Sexually Abused
✔ Mini-lecture: How Children Cope with Sexual Abuse Trauma and the Feelings That Result
✔ Exercise Two: Coping with Sexual Abuse/Incest as a Child and as an Adult

SESSION 6: ADULT SURVIVOR ISSUES: SELF-PERCEPTIONS

✔ Opening the Session
✔ Exercise One: Negative Self-Perceptions of the Sexually Abused Child and Adult Survivor
✔ Mini-lecture: The Distorted Self-Image—Negative Self-Perceptions of the Sexually Abused Child and the Adult Survivor
✔ Exercise Two: Changing the Distorted Image—Positive Affirmations
✔ Mini-lecture: Changing the Distorted Message—Affirmations, Boundaries, Self-Care, and Self-Nurturing
✔ Exercise Three: Affirmations, Boundaries, Self-Care, and Self-Nurturing

SESSION 7: ADULT SURVIVOR ISSUES: LEARNED ROLES AND RELATIONS WITH OTHERS

✔ Opening the Session
✔ Mini-lecture: Family Roles and Their Effect on the Sexually Abused Child and the Adult Survivor
✔ Exercise One: Roles in Your Family
✔ Exercise Two: Effects of Childhood Roles in Childhood and in Adulthood

✔ Mini-lecture: The Impact of Roles, Self-Esteem, and Abuse on Relationships
✔ Exercise Three: Examining Current Relationships

SESSION 8: SUPPORTIVE PEOPLE, SUPPORT NETWORKS, AND OTHER RESOURCES FOR RECOVERY

✔ Opening the Session
✔ Mini-lecture: Identifying Supportive People
✔ Exercise One: Safe/Trustworthy versus Unsafe/Untrustworthy People
✔ Mini-lecture: Value of a Support Network
✔ Exercise Two: Assessing Your Current Support Network
✔ Mini-lecture: Professionals and Peer Support Groups
✔ Closing and Evaluation

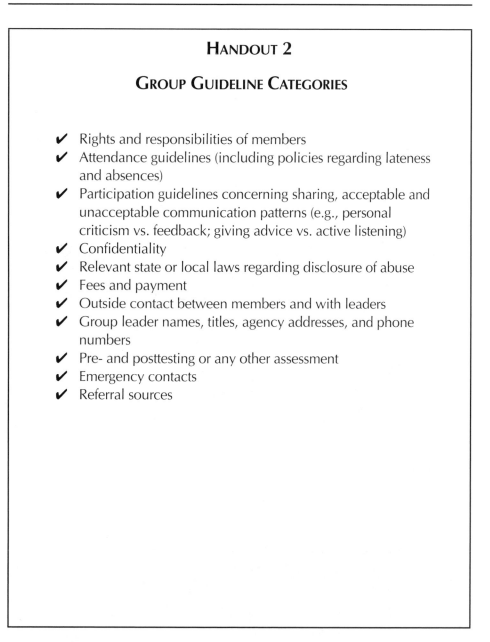

HANDOUT 2

GROUP GUIDELINE CATEGORIES

- ✔ Rights and responsibilities of members
- ✔ Attendance guidelines (including policies regarding lateness and absences)
- ✔ Participation guidelines concerning sharing, acceptable and unacceptable communication patterns (e.g., personal criticism vs. feedback; giving advice vs. active listening)
- ✔ Confidentiality
- ✔ Relevant state or local laws regarding disclosure of abuse
- ✔ Fees and payment
- ✔ Outside contact between members and with leaders
- ✔ Group leader names, titles, agency addresses, and phone numbers
- ✔ Pre- and posttesting or any other assessment
- ✔ Emergency contacts
- ✔ Referral sources

This handout is optional but recommended. It should be adapted to include the applicable policies and procedures of the agency or practice and to communicate state law requirements regarding confidentiality. Suggested categories for inclusion are listed above.

HANDOUT 3

SUGGESTED READING LIST

Baldwin, M. (1988). *Beyond victim: You can overcome childhood abuse . . . even sexual abuse!* Moore Haven, FL: Rainbow Books.

Bass, E., & Thornton, L. (Eds.). (1983). *I never told anyone: Writing by women survivors of child sexual abuse.* New York: Harper & Row.

Bass, E., & Davis, L. (1988). *The courage to heal: A guide for women survivors of child sexual abuse.* New York: Harper & Row.

Black, C. (1990). *Double duty.* New York: Ballantine Books.

Blume, E. (1990). *Secret survivors: Uncovering incest and its aftereffects in women.* New York: John Wiley and Sons.

Cohen, B., Giller, E., Lynne, W. (Eds.) (1991). *Multiple personality disorder from the inside out.* Baltimore, MD: The Sidran Press.

Courtois, C. (1988). *Healing the incest wound: Adult survivors in therapy.* New York: W. W. Norton.

Daugherty, L. (1984). *Why me? Help for victims of child sexual abuse (even if they are adults now).* Racine, WI: Mother Courage Press.

Davis, L. (1991). *Allies in healing: When the person you love was sexually abused as a child.* New York: Harper & Row.

Donaldson, M. (1983). *Incest, years after: Putting the pain to rest.* Fargo, ND: The Village Family Service Center.

Engel, B. (1989). *The right to innocence: Healing the trauma of childhood sexual abuse.* Los Angeles: Tarcher.

Forward, S. (1989). *Toxic parents: Overcoming their hurtful legacy and reclaiming your life.* New York: Bantam Books.

Gannon, J. (1989). *Soul survivors: A new beginning for adults abused as children.* Englewood Cliffs, NJ: Prentice-Hall.

Gil, E. (1984). *Outgrowing the pain.* San Francisco: Launch Press.

Jarvis-Kirkendall, C., & Kirkendall, J. (1989). *Without consent: How to overcome childhood sexual abuse.* Scottsdale, AZ: Swan Press.

Maltz, W. (1991). *The sexual healing journey.* New York: Harper/Collins.

Maltz, W., & Holman, B. (1987). *Incest and sexuality.* Lexington, MA: Lexington Books.

Mellody, P. (1989). *Facing codependence.* New York: Harper & Row.

Poston, C., & Lison, K. (1989). *Reclaiming our lives: Hope for adult survivors of incest.* Boston: Little, Brown & Co.

Ratner, E. (1990). *The other side of the family: A book for recovery from abuse, incest, and neglect.* Deerfield Beach, FL: Health Communications.

Rush, F. (1980). *The best kept secret: Sexual abuse of children.* Englewood Cliffs, NJ: Prentice-Hall.

Sisk, S., & Hoffman, C. F. (1987). *Inside scars: Incest recovery as told by a survivor and her therapist.* Gainesville, FL: Pandora Press.

Summit, R. (1983). The child sexual abuse accommodation syndrome. *Child Abuse and Neglect, 7,* 177–193.

Terr, L. (1990). *Too scared to cry: Psychic trauma in childhood.* New York: Harper & Row.

Tower, C. (1988). *Secret scars: A guide for survivors of child sexual abuse.* New York: Viking.

Wisechild, L. (1988). *The obsidian mirror: An adult healing from incest.* Seattle, WA: Seal Press.

Wood, M., & Hatton, L. (1989). *Triumph over darkness: Understanding and healing the trauma of childhood sexual abuse.* Hillsboro, OR: Beyond Words Publishing.

WORKBOOKS

Barnes, P. (1989). *The woman inside: A resource guide designed to lead women from incest victim to survivor.* Racine, WI: Mother Courage Press.

Davis, L. (1990). *The courage to heal workbook.* New York: Harper & Row.

Donaldson, M., & Green, S. (1987). *Incest, years after: Learning to cope successfully.* Fargo, ND: The Village Family Service Center.

Mellody, P., & Miller, A. (1989). *Breaking free: A recovery workbook for facing code-pendence.* New York: Harper & Row.

Nestingen, S., & Lewis, L. (1990). *Growing beyond abuse: A workbook for survivors of sexual exploitation or childhood sexual abuse.* Minneapolis, MN: Omni Recovery.

Whitfield, C. (1989). *A gift to myself: A personal workbook and guide to healing my child within.* Deerfield Beach, FL: Health Communications.

Wiseman, A. (1986, 1989). *Nightmare help.* Berkeley, CA: Ten Speed Press.

MALE SURVIVORS

Bolton, F., Jr., Morris, L., & MacEachron, A. (1989). *Males at risk: The other side of child sexual abuse.* Newbury Park, CA: Sage Publications.

Hunter, M. (1990). *Abused boys: The neglected victims of sexual abuse.* Lexington, MA: D. C. Heath.

Lew, M. (1988). *Victims no longer: Men recovering from incest and other sexual child abuse.* New York: Nevraumont.

SESSION 2
THE CONTEXT OF SEXUAL ABUSE:
FAMILY RULES AND DYSFUNCTION

OBJECTIVES

✔ To increase members' awareness of the context of sexual abuse, especially the family dysfunction found in incestuous families

✔ To clarify differences between functional and dysfunctional families

✔ To increase members' awareness of the rules of the dysfunctional family

✔ To help members understand the rules that operated in their families of origin

I. OPENING THE SESSION

A. Review Session 1. Ask members if they wish to comment on the content of the previous week's session.

B. Brief overview of Session 2.

II. MINI-LECTURE: THE FAMILY— FROM FUNCTIONAL TO DYSFUNCTIONAL

Families run the gamut from those that are highly functional and healthy to those that are highly dysfunctional or unhealthy. Some primary characteristics have been identified that distinguish healthy from unhealthy families. The "Family Continuum" handout places different types of families on a continuum in order to compare and contrast them. The handout shows dysfunctional modes of family functioning at the poles and more functional modes in the middle range. Most families are neither completely healthy nor completely unhealthy; rather, families show a blend of characteristics that can be identified as being weighted one way or the other.

In general, the functional family fosters respect for the child's individuality and development, responds appropriately to the child's needs, has a healthy concern for the child's welfare, and sets reasonable rules and expectations within which the child is taught to operate. These rules and expectations are somewhat flexible; they change and develop as the child matures and becomes more responsible and independent. The functional family operates in the middle ground between the poles of neglecting and abusing the child on the one hand and overprotecting and intruding upon the child on the other.

The dysfunctional family, however, has little or no respect or empathy for the developing child. The child's individuality is instead disregarded or stifled. Unreasonable rules and expectations prevail, which are often "out of sync" with the child's age and stage of development. These rules are inconsistently applied and enforced. The family atmosphere is frequently characterized by criticism and rejection, with little teaching or nurturance. For example, children are expected to be able to perform "beyond their years" without benefit of instruction or coaching. When performance does not meet the standards established by the parent, children are subject to harsh criticism, ridicule, and rejection. The dysfunctional family may alternate between the two poles of the continuum, that is, between overprotection and intrusiveness on one end (smothering the child) and neglect and abuse on the other. The family seldom operates within the middle ground.

Review the characteristics of a functional family and those of a dysfunctional family. Distribute the "Characteristics of a Healthy, Functional Family" and "Characteristics of an Unhealthy, Dysfunctional Family" handouts. Ask members if they have any questions or comments.

III. EXERCISE ONE: HOW FAMILY DYSFUNCTION CAN CONTRIBUTE TO SEXUAL ABUSE BOTH INSIDE AND OUTSIDE THE FAMILY AND HOW HEALTHY FAMILY FUNCTIONING WORKS AGAINST ABUSE

A. Objective: To increase members' awareness of how patterns of dysfunction might facilitate the occurrence of sexual abuse within and outside the family.

B. Break participants into groups of three or four. Instruct them to choose members with whom they have not yet worked.

C. Ask participants to discuss the following:

1. Three characteristics of dysfunctional families that contribute most to sexual abuse.
2. Three characteristics of functional families that most reduce the likelihood of sexual abuse.
3. Each small group discusses the chosen characteristics one at a time, then presents these to the larger group when it reconvenes.

D. Summarize the discussions in the large group.

E. Leaders list some of the primary findings on the flip chart and tie responses into the following mini-lecture.

IV. MINI-LECTURE: HOW DYSFUNCTION CONTRIBUTES TO SEXUAL ABUSE INSIDE AND OUTSIDE THE FAMILY

Dysfunctional families often have multiple problems: alcoholism, substance abuse, or other addictions; shame, denial, and family secrets; boundary problems inside and outside the family; role reversal between parent and child; rigid roles, abandonment, and rejection anxiety; sibling rivalry; perfectionism and codependence; workaholism; and internal chaos. Some of these families appear "normal" from the outside and work hard to maintain a facade of respectability. Others are in constant upheaval, equally chaotic in function and appearance.

Problem patterns are often found across generations. For example, secrets may be kept to protect against shame and humiliation. As a result, family shame is transmitted from one generation to the next without having a specific context. This kind of shame is at the root of much individual and family dysfunction, undergirding family rules that family secrets must not be revealed or family matters must not be discussed with outsiders. Denial and dishonesty are valued in the family, often unwittingly or unconsciously. Family rules keep family members in denial and from acknowledging family problems that are considered shameful (e.g., alcoholism; illegitimacy; illegal activities; abortion; debt; and sexual, physical, or emotional abuse).

The rigidity that characterizes these families shows up in their relational patterns. Family members are often very enmeshed. The family strives to keep individual members from becoming different in any significant way. Members receive positive reinforcement for compliance with family norms and negative reinforcement for noncompliance, independence, and breaking away. They are not respected for their uniqueness nor are they encouraged to pursue idiosyncratic talents and interests if doing so causes a change in the family *status quo*. Change and growth are threats to these families and are discouraged. Contacts and ties outside the family circle are also discouraged. Members are encouraged to rely only on one another, thus reinforcing internal dependence and desertion anxiety as well as isolation from the larger community. "Outsiders" are seen as threatening and untrustworthy—they are not kin and are therefore suspect.

Parents in dysfunctional families were often subject to this same type of upbringing. In all likelihood, they were abused in some way in childhood and reached adulthood in a shame-bound state with many unmet needs. Many of these individuals have difficulty relating positively with others. A strained marriage or relationship is common, characterized by communication problems, power struggles, and sexual difficulties.

As parents, these individuals may revert to what they learned in childhood, including the expectation that *their* children will meet *their* needs, especially those that are not being met by their spouse or partner. Role reversal or "parentification" of the child is quite common in these families. The child learns to take care of the parent and often the other children as well. This is best exemplified in families in which one or both parents are alcoholic and in which the child is pressed into making meals, budgeting, doing laundry, and so forth. Children in such families learn that love is not available or given freely by the parents, but rather is conditional on meeting the needs of others and on being pleasing. Despite this conditional acceptance and love, family members are required above all to be loyal. Thus denial is reinforced; members are discouraged from having outside contacts with or being influenced by outsiders.

V. MINI-LECTURE: COMMON RULES AND NEGATIVE MESSAGES IN DYSFUNCTIONAL FAMILIES

Dysfunctional families have rigid rules and negative messages that enforce the family mode of functioning. Family members are taught to incorporate and operate within the context of these rules and messages, which convey information about the family, relationships, and the identity and worth of each individual member. These rules are internalized to the point that they function automatically and outside the individual's awareness. To change these rules and negative messages, the individual must become aware of them. See the "Negative Rules and Messages in Troubled Families" handout.

VI. EXERCISE TWO: HOW FAMILY RULES AND MESSAGES SUPPORT SEXUAL ABUSE

A. Objective: To increase members' awareness of rigid rules and negative messages that support sexual abuse within or outside the family.

B. Assign members to triads, again with participants with whom they have not yet worked.

C. Leaders tape several lists of rigid rules or negative messages on the walls. Participants are asked to move about the room and to make a single checkmark next to rules or messages that apply to their family. After participants have had time to circulate, ask them to recirculate and this time make two checkmarks next to the rigid rule or negative message that was most often enforced or used in their family.

D. Participants form triads to discuss the rules and negative comments they checked, along with how their family enforced rules that were broken.

E. Summarize discussion in the large group.

F. Leaders should list some of the main considerations and findings on the board, tying in responses with the following mini-lecture.

VII. MINI-LECTURE: HOW RIGID FAMILY RULES AND NEGATIVE MESSAGES SUPPORT SEXUAL ABUSE WITHIN AND OUTSIDE THE FAMILY

Rigid rules and negative messages adversely affect how a child feels about him- or herself. Many of these rules and messages are presented in absolute, either/or language. They involve many "don't" and "always" messages: don't be, don't feel, don't trust, don't ask, don't expect and always be in control, always maintain the *status quo*, always be loyal, always deny, always cover up. The net effect of these rules is that the child feels worthless and unlovable or only as good as his or her behavior or performance. The child is taught to disregard personal reactions and feelings, especially when they contradict the rules and thus threaten the parent or the *status quo*. Negative injunctions are often used to discourage the child from independent thought and action and from seeking assistance. For example, "You wouldn't feel that if you really loved me" or "You should be ashamed of yourself" or "You're so selfish/stupid/worthless" or "You're to blame and shouldn't expect assistance."

These rules and messages put the child at risk for sexual abuse within and outside the family. The child with shaky self-esteem can easily be coerced or otherwise influenced by promises of special attention. The child trapped in ongoing sexual abuse, over time, blames him- or herself for its occurrence. If the child attempts disclosure, if the abuse is overt, if it is discovered and then disregarded, or if the child is blamed for the abuse, feelings of self-blame and self-hatred are reinforced. Moreover, without assistance or validation, the child may learn to deny, split off, or compartmentalize the abuse. These coping methods allow the child to deal with the contradictions in his or her environment.

With regard to incest, the following points are significant:

✔ Incestuous families often include parents who are alcoholic or otherwise unavailable and who are therefore unable to offer emotional support or nurturance to their children. In incestuous families, the parents' relationship is often strained. This strain extends to the children.

✔ Sexual contact may take the place of other forms of nurturance and positive touch. Dysfunctional families are often inconsistent in their nurturing. Children may be starved for positive physical contact.

✔ Children caught in incest often learn that abuse is the price of being loved and that sex is a commodity.

✔ Children in incestuous families are often caught in loyalty binds among family members. They keep the secret out of fear, anxiety, loyalty, or to protect others.

✔ Children in incestuous families often have to function beyond their maturity level, sometimes assuming the role of the parent to other family members (including the parents). Incest is a glaring example of this interaction style; the child is forced to function sexually as an adult, often as a replacement for an adult family member.

✔ In fulfilling the role of parent/spouse to other family members, the child's own emotional and physical needs go unmet.

✔ Many children who are incestuously abused keep the secret because they are afraid of being blamed, shamed, punished, abandoned, or rejected.

✔ Children who are incestuously abused often worry about the abuse, other family problems, and other family members. Such worrying uses up emotional energy, diverting it from other tasks, such as schoolwork, social activities, and so forth.

✔ In incestuous families, children are often encouraged to trust only other family members. This rule makes the child loyal and dependent on the family and likely to keep the secret in order to protect him- or herself and to avoid abandonment.

With regard to sexual abuse perpetrated outside the family, the following points are significant:

✔ Although sexual abuse that occurs outside the family does not trap the child as completely as does incest, many children are afraid to disclose what happened out of shame and fear.

✔ Abuse by strangers sometimes involves more force and more threats than does abuse by relatives (especially for male victims). This may make disclosure more difficult.

✔ Even with threats and increased force, abuse by a stranger is easier to report to the family because divided loyalty is not involved.

✔ Parents who learn of abuse outside the family are more likely to believe and protect their children; however, boys may be blamed more than girls (boys are supposed to be able to protect themselves) and thus may receive less assistance and support.

✔ Some children are sexually abused outside the family because they are sexually and/or physically abused and neglected within the family. Family abuse and neglect, as well as problems such as parental alcoholism, put children more at risk for abuse of any type.

✔ Children raised in troubled families often have low self-esteem and develop the habit of trying to please adults to obtain attention and nurturance. Such children are vulnerable to the influence of any adult who gives them attention, even when the attention involves abuse as a trade-off.

✔ When parents are alcoholic or otherwise uninvolved with or unresponsive to their children, children are reluctant to seek them out for assistance. Such children may have had previous painful experiences with regard to their parents' responses to problems.

Ask participants if they have any questions before closing the session.

BIBLIOGRAPHY

Bass, E., & Davis, L. (1988). *The courage to heal.* New York: Harper & Row.

Bradshaw, J. (1988). *Bradshaw on the family.* Deerfield Beach, FL: Health Communications.

Courtois, C. (1988). *Healing the incest wound: Adult survivors in therapy.* New York: W. W. Norton.

Ratner, E. (1990). *The other side of the family: A book for recovery from abuse, incest and neglect.* Deerfield Beach, FL: Health Communications.

Whitfield, C. (1989). *A gift to myself: A personal workbook and guide to healing my child within.* Deerfield Beach, FL: Health Communications.

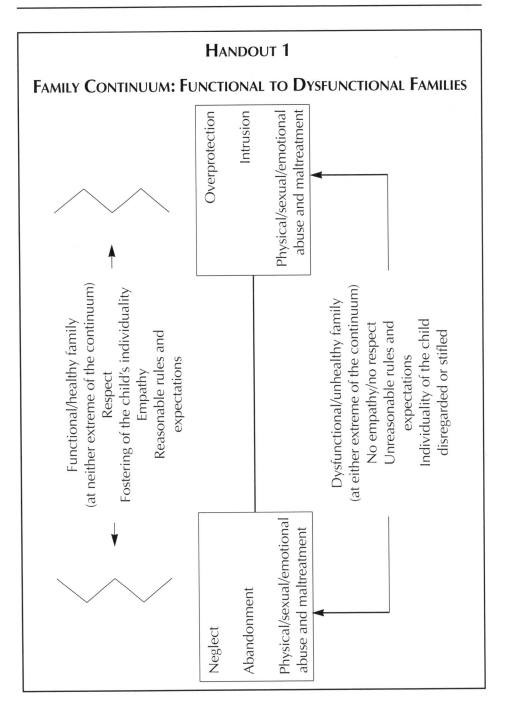

HANDOUT 1

FAMILY CONTINUUM: FUNCTIONAL TO DYSFUNCTIONAL FAMILIES

Overprotection

Intrusion

Physical/sexual/emotional abuse and maltreatment

Functional/healthy family
(at neither extreme of the continuum)
Respect
Fostering of the child's individuality
Empathy
Reasonable rules and expectations

Dysfunctional/unhealthy family
(at either extreme of the continuum)
No empathy/no respect
Unreasonable rules and expectations
Individuality of the child disregarded or stifled

Neglect

Abandonment

Physical/sexual/emotional abuse and maltreatment

HANDOUT 2

CHARACTERISTICS OF A HEALTHY, FUNCTIONAL FAMILY

Each member of the family is respected for his or her uniqueness and has equal value as a person.

Each member of the family is encouraged to develop as a unique individual. Family members can be different from one another and are not pressured to conform.

Parents do what they say and are consistent. They are good role models.

Communication is direct, and honesty among members is encouraged.

Family members are taught to develop and express their feelings, perceptions, needs, etc.

When problems develop, they are discussed and solutions are developed. Major problems such as alcoholism, compulsions, or abuse do not go unacknowledged or untreated.

Family members can get their needs met in the family.

Family roles are flexible.

Family rules are flexible, but accountability is required.

Violation of the rights or values of others causes guilt. Family members own their personal behavior and its consequences.

Learning is encouraged; mistakes are forgiven and viewed as part of the learning process.

The family is not completely closed in its internal interactions, nor is it completely open to the outside world.

The family supports each individual member.

Parents are not infallible and all-powerful; they negotiate and are reasonable in their interactions.

Adapted from Bradshaw, J. (1988). *Bradshaw on the family*. Deerfield Beach, FL: Health Communications.

HANDOUT 3

CHARACTERISTICS OF AN UNHEALTHY, DYSFUNCTIONAL FAMILY

Members are not respected as unique individuals of equal value with other family members.

Family members are discouraged from being unique or different from others in the family. Conformity is often required.

Parents do not follow through and are inconsistent. They are not good role models.

Communication is discouraged, as is honesty. Denial and deceit prevail.

Family members are denied their individual feelings, perceptions, and needs.

When problems develop, they are kept hidden, and the member with the problem is shamed into silence. Major problems are denied and thus continue unabated. Members are encouraged to show a happy face to the world.

Family members' needs go unmet in the family. Asking for favors or to have needs met is discouraged.

Family roles are rigid and inflexible.

Family rules are rigid and infractions are either ignored or severely punished. Responses are inconsistent.

Family members are continuously blamed and shamed; they do not comfortably own their personal behavior and its consequences.

Mistakes are severely criticized. Family members are expected to be always "right" or "perfect." Family members are not taught—they must learn on their own and expect criticism if they don't "get it right."

The family is overly open in members' internal interactions or overly closed to the outside world.

The family inconsistently supports individual members; however, individual support of the family is expected at all times.

Parents are infallible and all-powerful. They teach the child that they are always in control and are not to be questioned or challenged. Children do not have the right to disagree.

Adapted from Bradshaw, J. (1988). *Bradshaw on the family.* Deerfield Beach, FL: Health Communications.

HANDOUT 4

NEGATIVE RULES AND MESSAGES IN TROUBLED FAMILIES

Negative Rules

Don't express your feelings
Don't get angry
Don't get upset
Don't cry
Do as I say, not as I do
Be good, "nice," perfect
Avoid conflict (or avoid dealing with conflict)
Don't think or talk; just follow directions
Do well in school
Don't ask questions
Don't betray the family
Don't discuss the family with outsiders; keep the "family secret"
Be seen, not heard!
No back talk
Don't contradict me
Always look good
I'm always right; you're always wrong
Always be in control
Focus on the alcoholic's drinking (or troubled person's behavior)
Drinking (or other troubled behavior) is not the cause of our problems
Always maintain the status quo

Negative Messages

Shame on you
You're not good enough
I wish I'd never had you
Your needs are not all right with me
Hurry up and grow up
Be dependent
Be a man
Big boys don't cry
Act like a nice girl (or a lady)
You don't feel that way
Don't be like that
You're so stupid (or bad, etc.)
You caused it
You owe it to us
Of course, we love you!
I'm sacrificing myself for you
How can you do this to me?
We won't love you if you . . .
You're driving me crazy!
You'll never accomplish anything
It didn't really hurt
You're so selfish
You'll be the death of me yet
That's not true
I promise (though breaks it)
You make me sick
You're so stupid
We wanted a boy/girl

SESSION 3
CHILD SEXUAL ABUSE AS TRAUMA

OBJECTIVES

✔ To define trauma and post-traumatic stress reactions

✔ To describe primary factors of child sexual abuse that are traumatic

✔ To describe secondary factors of child sexual abuse that are traumatic

✔ To define other factors that dilute or modulate traumatic stress reactions

I. OPENING THE SESSION

A. Review Session 2. Ask group members if they have questions, comments, or reactions to Session 2 materials.

B. Overview of Session 3.

II. MINI-LECTURE: WHAT IS TRAUMA AND WHAT ARE POST-TRAUMATIC STRESS REACTIONS?

Stress is part of everyday life. It occurs as a response to stressor events and circumstances. A stress response is positive when it motivates, challenges, or excites an individual. It is negative (distress) when it deters, depresses, or exhausts an individual. Similar stressors can affect different people in varied ways, depending on their innate resilience, the meaning they attach to the stressor, other stressful events in their lives, their support system, and so forth.

When stress feels overwhelming, most individuals respond in one of three ways: fight, flight, or freeze. They either fight back, try to get away, or are paralyzed and unable to act. Stress management strategies have been developed to assist individuals in maintaining optimal levels of stress so that the "fight, flight, freeze" mechanism is not activated.

Trauma involves stress, but not on the same order of magnitude as ordinary life stress. A traumatic event is out of the ordinary, catastrophic, and, by definition, overwhelming. According to Lenore Terr, an authority on psychic trauma in children,

> "Psychic trauma" occurs when a sudden, unexpected, overwhelmingly intense emotional blow or a series of blows assaults the person from outside. Traumatic events are external, but they quickly become incorporated into the mind. A person probably will not become fully traumatized unless s/he feels utterly helpless during the event of events.[1]

Traumatic stress reactions are the first indicators of the presence of trauma and are natural emotions and behaviors in response to catastrophe, its immediate aftermath, and memories of it. These reactions can occur anytime after the trauma, even decades later. When a reaction is an immediate response, it is called acute; when it persists over time, it is called chronic; and when it develops later, it is called delayed. Some traumatized individuals react in all three ways.

Post-traumatic stress reactions (referred to as post-traumatic stress disorder when reactions are severe and persist over time) include three major sets of symptoms: (1) avoidance of anything that reminds the person of the event; (2) numbing of emotional responsiveness; and (3) increased arousal and responsiveness to anything reminiscent of the event. It should be noted that these reactions parallel the "fight, flight, freeze" reactions, although they are intensified. The "Characteristics of Post-Traumatic Stress Reactions" handout describes some common reactions.

III. EXERCISE ONE: CHARACTERISTICS OF POST-TRAUMATIC STRESS REACTIONS

A. Objective: To increase members' knowledge of the characteristics of post-traumatic stress reactions.

B. Leaders explain the characteristics of post-traumatic stress reactions as described in the handout and encourage participants to enter into discussion.

C. Ask group members if they have any questions.

IV. MINI-LECTURE: WHAT MAKES SEXUAL ABUSE OR INCEST TRAUMATIC FOR THE CHILD?

Traumatic stress reactions in children are similar to those exhibited by adults. However, adults are not as vulnerable and immature as children, which affects the intensity of their respective reactions. The trauma, by virtue of its occurrence later in life, does not affect the adult's personal development during his or her formative years as it does for child victims. Adults have a greater capacity to understand and verbalize the trauma and to organize their reactions than do children. However, adults do experience overwhelming feelings and can have a full range of post-traumatic reactions. In fact, trauma can cause adults to reexperience feelings of helplessness or dependence that characterized their childhood. In adulthood, these feelings can be very disorienting.

In the absence of fully developed emotional, verbal, physical, and cognitive capacities, children express their reactions through behavior as well as through indirect, symbolic forms such as dreams and play. The ability to communicate directly is affected by the child's age, stage of development, and level of maturity. Often, the child's play, artwork, fantasy life, dreams and nightmares, and relations with others express reactions in coded fashion. For example, a child's drawing might symbolically portray abuse as well as reactions to it. A child might be drawn as tiny in comparison with adults in the family. The child might eliminate the mouth in a picture of him- or herself, conveying powerlessness, secrecy, and forced silence.

The severity of the child's reaction to abuse depends on the age of the child at onset; the duration, frequency, and progression of the sexual activity over time; and the relationship between the child and the abuser. Although sexual child abuse is not always traumatic for every victim, the experience has high potential to traumatize.

Researchers David Finkelhor and Angela Browne have identified four main trauma-inducing factors in child sexual abuse (or what they call *traumagenic* factors): (1) *traumatic sexualization*, (2) *betrayal*, (3) *powerlessness*, and (4) *stigma*. These four factors operate together to create a specific childhood trauma that is different from trauma such as the divorce of a child's parents or even physical abuse. These factors alter the child's cognitive and emotional development. They create trauma by causing distortions in the child's sense of self and sense of others as well as his or her emotional development and perspective on the world and sense of safety in it.

Traumatic sexualization refers to the fact that in sexual abuse the child is sexualized at an age when he or she is physically and emotionally immature and in a way that is relationally dysfunctional. The child's sexuality is used to satisfy the needs of the abuser.

Betrayal refers to the child being deliberately used and harmed by someone on whom he or she is dependent and from whom protection and nurturance should be expected. Betrayal is usually most traumatic when the abuser is a parent. The intensity of reaction to betrayal declines thereafter according to the degree of closeness and relatedness between the child and abuser and the role the adult plays in the child's life.

Powerlessness refers to the child's helplessness and inability to do anything to prevent or stop the abuse.

Stigmatization refers to the negative connotations that are communicated to the child by the abuse, which then become incorporated into the developing child's sense of self: badness, shame, guilt, self-blame, and self-hatred.

In addition to these four, other factors have been found to be related to severity of abuse. Refer to the "Factors Related to Severity of Traumatic Stress Reaction" handout.

V. EXERCISE TWO: DISCUSSION OF SEXUAL ABUSE/INCEST FACTORS

A. Objective: To generate discussion about factors common to sexual abuse/incest, traumatic impact, and severity of reaction.

B. After these factors are explained by the leaders, they are posted in several places around the room. Participants mill around the room, noting reasons they think each factor is particularly traumatic for the child. Group members then reconvene for a full group discussion of the traumagenic factors and members' opinions on the trauma potential of each.

C. Ask group members if they have questions.

VI. MINI-LECTURE: FACTORS RELATED TO SECONDARY STRESS REACTIONS; PROTECTIVE FACTORS THAT MODERATE OR MODULATE THE TRAUMA

Other aspects of sexual abuse, especially incest, can result in more serious or compounded reactions. Mary Ann Donaldson describes two levels of stressors in incest: the *primary stressor*, which is the sexual abuse itself, and the *secondary stressor*, which refers to the context in which it occurs. The primary stressor causes the initial post-traumatic stress reactions. The secondary stressors include the context of abuse: being around the abuser on a regular basis; being around other family members; forced silence and maintaining secrecy; isolation during the abuse and afterward; anything having to do with sex, dating, and feelings of self-blame, guilt, shame, and confusion. Secondary stress reactions result from the atmosphere and psychological needs created by the primary factors. Because the child can never really get away from the incest and his or her feelings about it, the secondary reactions get very complicated and cause symptoms such as depression, anxiety, etc. (Symptoms of abuse experience are discussed in Session 5.)

Finally, some factors within and outside the family have been found to moderate or dilute the negative effects of sexual abuse or incest. The "Protective Factors That Modulate or Dilute Traumatic Stress Reactions" handout lists these factors.

VII. EXERCISE THREE: FACTORS RELATED TO SECONDARY STRESS REACTIONS

A. Objective: To increase participants' awareness of the secondary traumatic factors and protective factors of incest.

B. The leaders engage the group in a full-group discussion of the secondary factors and the protective factors to increase understanding of how they work to compound or dilute traumatic stress reactions. Leaders ask members to discuss their thoughts about how different factors cause greater or lesser reactions to develop over time.

C. Before closing the session, ask group members if they have any questions.

NOTE

1. L. Terr (1990). *Too scared to cry: Psychic trauma in childhood.* New York: Harper & Row, p. 8.

BIBLIOGRAPHY

Courtois, C. (1988). *Healing the incest wound: Adult survivors in therapy.* New York: W. W. Norton.

Donaldson, M. (1983). *Incest, years after: Putting the pain to rest.* Fargo, ND: The Village Family Service Center.

Donaldson, M., & Greene, S. (1987). *Incest, years after: Learning to cope successfully.* Fargo, ND: The Village Family Service Center.

Finkelhor, D., & Browne, A. (1985). The traumatic impact of child sexual abuse: A conceptualization. *American Journal of Orthopsychiatry, 55,* 530–541.

Ratner, E. (1990). *The other side of the family: A book for recovery from abuse, incest, and neglect.* Deerfield Beach, FL: Health Communications.

Terr, L. (1990). *Too scared to cry: Psychic trauma in childhood.* New York: Harper & Row.

HANDOUT 1

CHARACTERISTICS OF POST-TRAUMATIC STRESS REACTIONS

Physical reactions to small stresses as if they were the original trauma.

Sleep and dream disturbances. People may sleep with their eyes open as if poised for flight. Symptoms may increase with changes in routine. For example, sleeping next to another person may cause a survivor to sleep fitfully. Dreams may be vivid and symbolic or they may be exact recreations of the abuse.

Irritability, extreme irritation and reaction to noise or minor stimulants.

Increase in the startle response.

Fixation on the trauma.

Explosive behavior and/or trouble modulating and controlling anger. Rage must be directed somewhere—either toward the self or against others. It sometimes manifests itself in physical illness.

Reduced ability to function. Some persons with post-traumatic stress disorder (PTSD) can function quite well. However, it has been shown that after PTSD is resolved, functioning increases.

Fantasy as a means to cope with stress.

Becoming a "career" patient, either physical or psychiatric.

Helplessness and passivity—the inability to look for and find solutions to problems.

Inability to differentiate among emotions.

Sensory (body) experiences.

Defensive over- or undercontrol of life events.

Trouble in forming attachments or increased idealization and/or hate of others.

Attachment to trauma. Attracted to relationships that resemble the traumatic relationship. Selecting television programs or movies in which people are victimized. Involvement with helping persons may end in attempts to become "one" with the helper or in total rejection of the helper. May vacillate between the two.

Self-blame and a sense of being tainted or evil. This reaction may be prevalent even in individuals who have experienced trauma at a later age and who understand the context of the abuse.

Abnormal electroencephalogram (EEG) indicating a brain wave abnormality may occur as a result of PTSD. Some research shows EEG abnormalities, as well as hysterical seizures, learning disabilities, and attentional disorders.

Adapted with permission from Ratner, E. (1990). *The other side of the family: A book for recovery from abuse, incest, and neglect.* Deerfield Beach, FL: Health Communications.

Handout 2

Factors Related to Severity of Traumatic Stress Reactions

Duration and frequency: Incest that occurs more frequently and is of longer duration is potentially more harmful than short-term, less frequent abuse.

Type of sexual activity: Sexual abuse involving penetration of any sort is potentially more harmful than that involving other forms of sexual behavior.

Age at onset: The influence of the child's age at onset of abuse has been debated. Some researchers predict that onset at a younger age causes more damage; others believe that younger age helps insulate the child and that older children suffer more damage.

Age, gender, and relationship of the perpetrator: The more closely related the victim and perpetrator and the wider age difference between them, the greater the potential damage. Also, abuse perpetrated by a male is believed to be more severe and therefore more damaging than that by a woman.

Passive submission or willing participation on the part of the child: The child who goes along with the wishes of the perpetrator and submits without struggle or who willingly participates suffers more negative effects in the long run. He or she is more likely to engage in self-blame while ignoring the abuse circumstances.

Overt or disclosed incest with lack of assistance: Lack of assistance after the incest is known or disclosed has more potential for damage than does incest that remains hidden.

Parental reaction: Negative parental reactions upon discovery or reporting of incest cause further trauma for the child.

Institutional response: Negative, stigmatizing response or ineffective assistance on the part of social service and law-enforcement agencies contributes to trauma.

Note: These factors are listed according to their likelihood, on average, to cause severe reactions. Individual reactions vary dramatically and do not always fit the average case.

Adapted from Courtois, C. (1988). *Healing the incest wound: Adult survivors in therapy.* New York: W. W. Norton.

HANDOUT 3

FACTORS THAT MODULATE OR DILUTE TRAUMATIC STRESS REACTIONS

Individual Factors

✔ Emotional hardiness or resilience: The ability to be optimistic and to bounce back.
✔ Self-esteem: A positive sense of self-worth.
✔ Personal power: Sometimes called internal locus of control. A measure of control over one's environment.
✔ Ability to relate well with others: Able to make friends and participate in social relationships.
✔ Intellectual or cognitive ability: Able to think about, understand, and find meaning in the events of one's life.

Family Factors

✔ Supportive and concerned about the child's well-being and happiness as a unique individual. Not punitive and critical.
✔ Family structure is clearly understood. Parents are in control and have well-defined roles as adults. Communication with and expectations of the child are consistent and geared to the child's age and level of understanding.
✔ Parent or other adult models healthy optimism, problem-solving, and coping skills.

Social Factors

✔ Social environment provides external support and recognition, which in turn bolster self-esteem and self-confidence.
✔ Psychosocial intervention is available to support or protect the child if needed.

Note: These factors are often present pretrauma; however, their influence may be undermined during and after the trauma.

This handout is derived in part from Donaldson, M., & Greene, S. (1987). *Incest, years after: Learning to cope successfully.* Fargo, ND: The Village Family Service Center.

SESSION 4
COMMON EFFECTS OF CHILD SEXUAL ABUSE

OBJECTIVES

✔ To help members understand the initial and long-term effects of child sexual abuse

✔ To help members understand how they or someone they know were affected by abuse in childhood and in adulthood

✔ To help members express their feelings about the effects of child sexual abuse on them or someone whom they know

✔ To help members develop perspective on the abuse and its effects

I. OPENING THE SESSION

A. Review Session 3. Ask members if they have questions or comments on the material presented in Session 3.

B. Brief overview of Session 4.

II. MINI-LECTURE: INITIAL EFFECTS OF CHILD SEXUAL ABUSE

Sexual abuse affects the child and later the adult personally and as they relate to others. Six main categories of initial and long-term effects (in addition to the post-traumatic stress reactions described in Session 3) have been identified in studies of sexually abused individuals.

A. *Emotional Reactions.* The most common emotional reactions include fear, anxiety, confusion, guilt, anger, shame, self-blame, depression, and loss. (See Session 5 handout—"Common Feelings of the Sexually Abused Child"—for a comprehensive list of feelings.) The child is usually unable to understand and work through these feelings and may express them indirectly through behavior and artwork.

B. *Self-Perceptions.* Sexually abused children often develop a negative perception of self associated with feelings of guilt and shame. They may feel different from others, stigmatized, isolated, and contaminated. Their behavior may be as "bad" as they feel or may compensate for their feelings by being good and pleasing. Both strategies may be coded cries for help.

C. *Physical Effects.* The following body symptoms and behaviors have been identified in sexually abused children: regression to less mature or developed behavior (i.e., bedwetting in a child who is already toilet trained, baby talk and thumb sucking, clinging behavior); sudden onset of aches and pains such as headaches, stomachaches, and genital or anal discomfort and pain; dissociation, fainting, and epileptic-like seizures; eating disturbances, including loss or gain of appetite and weight; signs of depression and anxiety, such as lethargy, inability to concentrate or study, rashes, and phobias; signs of physical and genital trauma and infection; pregnancy; perceptual disturbances; fear and terror reactions, such as gaze aversion, frozen watchfulness, speech and movement inhibition; the repetition of the trauma (either as victim or abuser) in dreams, fantasies, play, and interactions with others; and sudden behavioral or personality changes.

D. *Sexual Effects.* The abused child may show a range of sexual effects from abuse. The child may exhibit age-inappropriate awareness of or curiosity about sexual activities and engage in compulsive behavior such as masturbation and exhibitionism, repeated attempts to engage others (children and adults) in sex play, and sexually abusive behavior toward other (usually younger) children. Through these behaviors, the child attempts to resolve feelings, especially anxiety, about the sexual abuse, while exhibiting and discharging the sexual overstimulation.

Some children react in the opposite way, avoiding physical contact with others. Touch may be perceived as negative, disgusting, and hurtful. The child who believes or was told that his or her body caused the abuse or who experienced sexual arousal in response to the abuse may feel self-disgust and body alienation characterized by self-neglect and self-harm.

E. *Relations with Others.* Sexual abuse results in feelings of mistrust of, betrayal by, and disillusionment with others. Intimacy and closeness with others may be associated with the abuse experience. Many abused children are withdrawn, isolating themselves from others in an effort to ensure safety. Some children become hostile, aggressive, and uncontrollable. Others may become pleasing and overrespon-sive to the needs and moods of others. Children may become highly sexualized and relate sexually to other children and to adults.

F. *Social Functioning.* Social functioning ranges from highly func-tional to highly dysfunctional. Some children exhibit develop-mental delays and learning difficulties. Others become high achievers and pseudo mature in their functioning with peers and with adults.

III. EXERCISE ONE: PARTICIPANTS' AWARENESS OF INITIAL EFFECTS OF CHILD SEXUAL ABUSE

A. Objective: To increase participants' awareness of the initial effects of child sexual abuse for them or someone whom they know in the six categories described above.

B. Distribute the "Initial Effects of Child Sexual Abuse" handout; ask participants to spend approximately 15 minutes identifying ways in which they were affected.

C. Ask the group to break into dyads to discuss their responses.

D. Open the large group to questions, comments, or discussion.

IV. MINI-LECTURE: LONG-TERM EFFECTS OF CHILD SEXUAL ABUSE

Long-term effects develop or persist two or more years post-abuse. Acute initial reactions can become chronic, or reactions may be delayed years after the initial abuse. Some effects appear, then spontaneously disappear.

A. *Emotional Reactions.* The adult's initial emotional reactions to past sexual abuse (see Session 5 handout, "Common Feelings of the Sexually Abused Child") may fluctuate drastically. Common feelings include depression and anxiety as well as shame, guilt, self-blame, and confusion.

B. *Self-Perceptions.* The adult survivor's predominant view of self is often negative and bound by shame. Adults continue to ask themselves how and why the abuse happened to them. They feel fated and contaminated and are often in despair.

C. *Physical Effects.* Self-hatred and body-disgust may continue into adulthood. Some survivors become completely alienated from their bodies, abusing and depriving themselves of food and rest. All of the initial physical effects experienced by the child can continue into adulthood. Trauma affects both the mind and the body. In adulthood, anxiety and fear-related physical symptoms are common, including stomach disturbance, respiratory distress, gynecological problems, immunological disturbances, chronic pain, muscular tension, and stress reactions.

D. *Sexual Effects.* Sexual abuse strongly affects adult sexuality and sexual functioning. Three main categories of effects have been documented:

1. *Sexual behavior in adolescence and early adulthood.* Abuse survivors are "out of sync" with their sexual development as a

result of their early sexualization. Two predominant and contradictory sexual styles emerge in adolescence and early adulthood: (1) isolation and sexual abstinence and (2) a high degree of sexual activity (often indiscriminate). Some survivors alternate between these two modes. Many survivors have no difficulty with their sexual functioning until they enter a committed relationship. Commitment and attachment may trigger feelings of entrapment and heighten anxiety, which in turn interferes with sexual functioning.

2. *Sexual orientation and preference.* Both male and female survivors may be confused about their sexual orientation in the aftermath of abuse. Male survivors may be particularly confused because such abuse is often perpetrated by another man. They may fear or believe that they are homosexual. Female survivors of abuse by a male perpetrator may be so fearful of or "turned off" by men that they become unsure of their sexual identity and gender preference.

3. *Sexual arousal, response, and satisfaction difficulties.* Many sexual disturbances and dysfunctions can be traced to child sexual abuse. Such dysfunctions include sexual aversion, pain, desire disorder, arousal problems, and orgasmic difficulties, among others. Abuse does not automatically cause sexual dysfunction, however. Some adult survivors report no negative sexual consequences.

E. *Relations with Others.* Child sexual abuse can affect interpersonal relationships in adulthood:

1. *General relations with both men and women.* Mistrust of others is at the core of most interpersonal difficulties. Many survivors believe, "If I couldn't trust my parents or family, whom can I trust?" Adult survivors often relate to others in the prescribed ways and roles they learned in their families. Thus, they may have little or no opportunity to learn different modes of interacting. They often characterize their relationships as one-way, empty, superficial, guarded, idealized, conflictual, or sexualized.

2. *Intimate and committed relationships.* Because such relationships require trust and vulnerability, adult survivors experience intima-

cy as entrapping and threatening rather than satisfying. Some survivors are unable to establish intimate relationships. Some find partners who relate to them in ways that are familiar. Thus they end up in codependent, addictive, or other dysfunctional relationships in which they play out familiar roles.

3. *Family-of-origin relationships.* The conflicted relationship and prescribed roles with parents and siblings often continue into adulthood. Difficulties in the family of origin might also extend to relationships with in-laws and authority figures. Family-of-origin relationship patterns and unresolved difficulties are extended into adult relationships.

4. *Parenting.* Abuse adversely affects many adult survivors' ability to parent their own children adequately. Survivors may have little understanding of or skill in parenting. Unresolved sexual abuse may inhibit developing emotional bonds and physical closeness with children. On the other hand, some survivors are good, even exceptional, parents. They may be driven by determination not to let their children suffer what they suffered as children.

F. *Social Effects.* The social functioning of adult survivors shows wide variability, ranging from isolation, rebellion, and antisocial behavior to overfunctioning and compulsive social interactions. Some survivors are so damaged that they are unable to function and may be found among the chronically mentally ill, the unemployed, the disabled, and the homeless. Some live a life of alienation, rebelliousness, and deviance, engaged in chronic antisocial activities. Other survivors, however, function at a moderately high level and some function at a very high level.

Many adult survivors experience decreased functioning when they enter the mid-life transition of their late thirties and forties. They may be overtaken by delayed traumatic stress reactions. A recent, well-publicized example of this response was exhibited by the former Miss America, Marilyn Van Debur Atler. For years, her family, social, and occupational functioning were exemplary and in absolute control. During mid-life, however, memories of her abuse weakened long-held defenses and she was virtually unable to function.

V. Exercise Two: Participants' Awareness of Long-Term Effects of Child Sexual Abuse

A. Objective: To increase participants' awareness of the effects of sexual abuse on childhood and/or adult functioning according to the six categories described above.

B. Distribute the "Long-Term Effects of Child Sexual Abuse" handout. Ask members to take approximately 15 minutes to respond to these categories.

C. Ask members to pair up with another group member and discuss their responses for approximately 10 minutes.

D. Encourage comments, reactions, discussion, or questions in the large group.

VI. Exercise Three: Recognizing Strengths and Developing Perspective

A. Objectives

   1. To increase participants' awareness of their reactions to initial and long-term effects of child sexual abuse.
   2. To increase participants' awareness of their personal strengths in order to counterbalance negative aftereffects that have been identified in this session.
   3. To help members put the sexual abuse and its effects in perspective by identifying positive and negative influences.

B. Distribute the "Reactions to Exercises One and Two" handout. Ask participants to respond to the first set of questions.

C. Break the group into pairs to discuss their responses to the first set of questions (approximately 10 minutes).

D. Ask participants to respond to the second set of questions.

E. Ask participants to discuss their responses to these questions (approximately 10 minutes).

F. Ask participants to respond to the third set of questions.

G. Ask participants to discuss their responses to these questions (approximately 10 minutes).

H. Reassemble the large group and encourage discussion, comments, reactions, and questions.

I. Summarize the discussion and list relevant material on the flip chart or chalkboard.

J. Warn participants of the possibility of delayed reactions to the session material. Encourage them to reach out to their support system or to contact the leaders between sessions if their feelings become overly strong or uncomfortable.

BIBLIOGRAPHY

Atler, M. Van Debur (1991, June 10). The darkest secret. *People Magazine,* pp. 89–94.

Bass, E., & Davis, L. (1988). *The courage to heal: A guide for women survivors of child sexual abuse.* New York: Harper & Row.

Courtois, C. (1988). *Healing the incest wound: Adult survivors in therapy.* New York: W. W. Norton.

Davis, L. (1990). *The courage to heal workbook: For women and men survivors of child sexual abuse.* New York: Harper & Row.

HANDOUT 1

INITIAL EFFECTS OF CHILD SEXUAL ABUSE

Consider yourself or someone who you know was sexually abused as a child. Identify ways this person or you were affected during the abuse or in its immediate aftermath, according to the following six areas:

Emotional reactions (guilt, anger, shame, etc.)

_____

_____

_____

Self-perception (self-blame, sense of "badness," low self-esteem, etc.)

_____

_____

_____

Physical effects (pain, headaches, muscular tension, etc.)

_____

_____

_____

Sexual effects (arousal, compulsive interest, avoidance)

_____

_____

_____

Relations with others (distrust, avoidance, overdependence)

_____

_____

_____

Social functioning (overfunctioning, underfunctioning)

_____

_____

_____

HANDOUT 2

LONG-TERM EFFECTS OF CHILD SEXUAL ABUSE

Consider yourself or someone whom you know was sexually abused as a child. Identify ways you or that person experienced long-term effects, according to the following six areas:

Emotional reactions (guilt, anger, shame, etc.)

_____

_____

_____

Self-perception (self-blame, sense of "badness," low self-esteem, etc.)

_____

_____

_____

Physical effects (pain, headaches, muscular tension, etc.)

_____

_____

_____

Sexual effects (arousal, compulsive interest, avoidance)

_____

_____

_____

Relations with others (distrust, avoidance, overdependence)

_____

_____

_____

Social functioning (overfunctioning, underfunctioning)

_____

_____

_____

HANDOUT 3

REACTIONS TO EXERCISES ONE AND TWO

When I look over my responses, I feel

_____

_____

_____

_____

I've been most strongly affected in the area(s) of

_____

_____

_____

_____

I was least affected in the area(s) of

_____

_____

_____

_____

The hardest statements for me to acknowledge were:

✔ _____

✔ _____

✔ _____

✔ _____

✔ _____

I feel most hopeful about making changes in

_____

_____

_____

_____

I've already made major strides in the following areas:

_____

_____

_____

_____

I feel the most hopeless about changing

_____

_____

_____

_____

I was surprised by

_____

_____

_____

_____

I learned

_____

_____

_____

_____

Adapted with permission from Davis, L. (1990). *The courage to heal workbook: For women and men survivors of child sexual abuse.* New York: Harper & Row.

HANDOUT 4

IDENTIFYING STRENGTHS

Recognizing your strengths does not mean that you have to minimize your abuse or discount the negative effect it's had on your life. Rather, it's a way to feel good about yourself despite what happened to you. It's a way to recognize the abilities and qualities that enable you to heal.

Check the statements that apply to you. Add any other strengths that you can think of.

_____ I'm stubborn. I won't give up.
_____ I'm determined. When I set my mind to something, I persist.
_____ I won't let anyone abuse me anymore.
_____ I have empathy for other people in pain.
_____ I understand human suffering.
_____ If I lived through the abuse, I can live through anything.
_____ I don't have many illusions about the world. I see things as they are.
_____ I'm self-sufficient. I can take care of myself.
_____ I'm courageous.
_____ I'm perceptive and can figure out what's really going on.
_____ I know how to handle a crisis.
_____ I survived.
_____ I'm calm and patient.

_____ _____
_____ _____
_____ _____
_____ _____

If you weren't able to identify many (or any) strengths, you're not alone. Sometimes, when you're in a negative mood and feel bad about yourself, it's hard to recognize your strengths. But they are there. Otherwise, you wouldn't have survived. If you had a hard time with this exercise, come back to it later and try again. Or ask people close to you about the strengths they see in you.

Handout 5

Putting the Abuse in Perspective

After survivors begin to look at the long-term effects of abuse, they often state that everything they experience is a direct result of having been sexually abused. Although it's tempting to think this way, it usually isn't accurate. Although sexual abuse has long-lasting, severe effects, it is still only one of many factors that shaped you. For some survivors, it is by far the most pervasive influence. For others, growing up in a racist society, being adopted, living in poverty, or being the first child of five had equal or greater impact. In assessing the effects of abuse on your life, it's important to put the abuse in perspective with the other forces that shaped you.

Make a list of factors that most strongly influenced your development as a child. Include both positive and negative influences (for instance, my grandmother's love; growing up poor; learning to read; my football coach; my father's alcoholism; growing up Puerto Rican in a black neighborhood; being a twin; my love of music; or Miss Johnson, my fifth-grade teacher). Some items may have both positive and negative aspects. Sandwich them in the middle.

Positive influences

Negative influences

_____   _____

_____   _____

_____   _____

_____   _____

_____   _____

_____   _____

_____   _____

_____   _____

_____   _____

Look over the items on your list. Consider their influence on your life today. Then rank each item in order of importance on a scale of 1 to 3. The things that influenced you the most get a 1. The things that were the second most important influences get a 2, and so on. (You can give the same number value to more than one item.) When everything has a number, complete the following sentences.

The biggest factors affecting my development were

_____

_____

The positive influences that enabled me to survive were

_____

_____

A good influence I forgot about was

_____

_____

Compared with other influences, sexual abuse

_____

_____

I was surprised

_____

_____

I learned

_____

_____

You may wish to complete this exercise again later. As you continue to heal, the influence of sexual abuse on your present life will decrease. A year or two from now, you will probably evaluate things differently.

SESSION 5

COPING WITH THE AFTERMATH OF SEXUAL ABUSE TRAUMA IN CHILDHOOD AND ADULTHOOD

OBJECTIVES

✔ To help participants understand the feelings and emotional reactions of children who are sexually abused

✔ To help participants understand how children cope with both the ongoing trauma of sexual child abuse and with their feelings

✔ To help participants understand how adults cope with the past trauma of sexual child abuse and with their current feelings

✔ To help participants assess their coping strategies and the needs these strategies meet, and to replace unhealthy strategies with healthier mechanisms

I. OPENING THE SESSION

A. Review Session 4. Ask participants if they have questions or comments on the material of Session 4.

B. Brief overview of Session 5.

II. EXERCISE ONE: CHILDREN'S FEELINGS AFTER BEING SEXUALLY ABUSED

A. Objective: To increase participants' awareness of the feelings that children have while being sexually abused and in the aftermath of abuse.

B. Ask participants to respond individually to the statement on the "Feelings of a Sexually Abused Child" handout: "Imagine a child who is sexually abused repeatedly. List this child's feelings." Engage the full group in a discussion about their responses.

C. List participants' responses on the flip chart. Make sure that the feelings listed on the "Common Feelings of the Sexually Abused Child" handout are mentioned.

D. Go back over the list and ask participants to suggest aspects of the sexual abuse/incest that might result in these feelings. These factors are outlined in Sessions 2 and 3; this exercise reviews and reinforces the material presented in those sessions.

III. MINI-LECTURE: HOW CHILDREN COPE WITH CHILD SEXUAL ABUSE TRAUMA AND THE FEELINGS THAT RESULT

Children cope with ongoing sexual abuse trauma and resultant feelings in various ways. Coping or survival skills allow the child to endure the abuse until he or she can escape or until the abuse stops. Coping strategies may seem strange or excessive when they are considered out of context. In fact, many survivors later criticize themselves for the ways in which they coped.

Coping strategies and behaviors should be respected because they allow the child to survive a traumatic experience in the absence of help and against extreme odds. However, in adulthood and/or after the abuse has stopped, these survival mechanisms need to be assessed as to their continued effectiveness. Behaviors that once ensured survival may later become problematic. For example, a child might have learned to turn off all physical sensations in order to survive the pain of sexual abuse. This same survival mechanism can be dangerous if it causes the child (and later the adult) to remain unaware of body sensations and pain. It is noteworthy that the coping mechanisms children use are often consistent with the family rules and injunctions with which they have been raised. For example, children raised in famillies that discourage expression of feelings may become emotionally numb and withdrawn. They cope by not feeling their feelings or by keeping everything to themselves. Keep this in mind during the following discussion.

Some coping strategies develop into strengths and skills that serve the child and later the adult very well. These include:
✔ Self-sufficiency
✔ Heightened awareness of the needs and emotional states of others
✔ Development of specialized skills
✔ Persistence and tolerance
✔ A sense of humor
✔ Creativity

Other coping strategies (such as lying and manipulation, overcontrol, addictions, self-mutilation, emotional isolation) are self-defeating and self-damaging in the long run. They cripple the survivor both emotionally and in his or her general life functioning. A strategy can have both healthy and unhealthy effects. Recovery requires survivors to differentiate between the two. Strategies that are no longer useful can be identified and appreciated for their usefulness in the past. The survivor can then change to more adaptive strategies and behaviors.

Coping strategies can be considered as points on a continuum. They range from adaptations that are mild and used only occasionally on an as-needed basis (such as creating a brief fantasy or daydream to counter reality) to those that are major and used regularly (such as totally blocking out reality through amnesia or repression). The latter might become embedded in the developing child's personality. In this way, trauma coping responses become internalized and part of the personality.

Coping strategies are numerous and diverse. Some are highly individualized and develop out of the particular circumstances and the child's creativity and adaptability. Others are more universal. The following highlights those strategies that are commonly used. The "Common Coping Strategies of the Sexually Abused Child" handout lists these strategies. Keep in mind that the list is incomplete. Many others or variations of these may have been used.

A. *Psychological/Cognitive Coping Mechanisms*

1. *Inner wisdom.* In the face of chronic and escalating sexual violation and in the absence of assistance or nurturance, some children develop an inner voice or inner wisdom that essentially serves as an inner parent. This mechanism may continue into adulthood and provide the survivor with inner strength and self-nurturance.

2. *Denial and the distortion of self and personal reality.* Sexually abused children often learn that they must deny what is happening to them as well as their true selves and feelings. They must hide *who they really are* in an attempt to cope with the abuse and to maintain the love and approval of family members (who might even include the abuser). Children also deny their sexual abuse experiences (whether inside or outside the family) because they are ashamed of the abuse and mistakenly believe that *they caused* the abuse or that they were abused because they *deserved to be.* As the child denies and thus distorts the reality of the experience (or "forgets" it), the *true self is denied.* In its place, the child develops a *false self* (sometimes called the codependent self), which is distorted to meet the needs and expectations of others and is dependent upon outside approval for self-esteem and security. The false self is very much a "conditional self."

3. *Dissociative reactions.* Dissociation occurs when the survivor alters his or her identity, consciousness, and memory in some way. The world of the sexually abused child is distorted and confusing. The child copes by segmenting or splitting off conflicting aspects of consciousness, memory, and identity in order to make them psychologically manageable. A primary mechanism for altering reality involves *amnesia* or *blocking out of memory.* This reaction can be partial, selective, or total, depending on the strength of the stressor and the child's age at time of occurrence. Younger children subject to prolonged and/or forceful sexual abuse are more prone to severe memory disturbance or total repression.

Reality and identity splitting, another mechanism used to alter reality, allows the abused child to psychologically separate him- or herself from the abuse experience. Many adult survivors describe "spacing out," leaving the body, and watching themselves be abused. In this way, survivors develop a reality or identity outside the abuse. They may anesthetize themselves physically and emotionally, a process called *numbing.* Although these strategies begin during episodes of abuse and are initially under the child's control, over time they may become automatic, causing the child or adult to "space out" in response to any stressor. In such instances, the child or adult loses his or her sense of time, conscious reality, and self-control. The individual loses touch with the circumstances that caused this response.

4. *Other psychological adaptations.* Abused children generally reverse the responsibility for the abuse from the abuser to themselves. They minimize or rationalize how and why the abuse happened (e.g., "He was lonely or drunk." "It wasn't so bad—he only felt my breasts; at least he didn't rape me."). Through these rationalizations, the perpetrator is exonerated. However, survivors often incorporate the responsibility for the abuse and the messages it conveys into their personality and their beliefs about themselves. The survivor thus becomes deserving, bad, and so forth. Because the abuse experience is so entrapping, survivors learn that nothing they do makes any difference. Learned helplessness and hopelessness develop alongside extreme anger and frustration, which are often self-directed rather than directed toward the abuser and/or nonprotecting others.

Children also tend to use any available mechanism or opportunity to escape their psychological trauma: fantasy, television, video games, reading, hobbies, food, drugs, schoolwork, after-school activities. Compulsive *busyness* can become a way to block out a disturbing reality.

Finally, some children make deals or try to bargain either with themselves or with their abuser. They might tell themselves that the abuse is deserved or that it is a trade-off for special attention or favors. Or they might trade their own bodies in an effort to protect other children in the family. Such "deals" are disregarded by most abusers, which often signifies an additional betrayal for the child as well as another source of rage.

B.   *Physical Coping Mechanisms.* These may overlap with many of the psychological mechanisms described above, but may be freestanding as well.

1. *Personal negligence and self-harm.* Because children often blame themselves and because the body is the target of the abuse, self-hatred and contempt often occur. Many survivors direct their anger against themselves through self-neglect, through risk-taking activities and risky relationships, and through actual harm such as self-mutilation and suicide attempts. Many survivors never received adequate care in their families, nor were they taught appropriate self-care.

2. *Control of self and environment.* Many children respond to the lack of power and control experienced during abuse by excessively controlling themselves and their environment in other situations. They may become hyperalert to any hint of intrusion and may manipulate their environment in an effort to make it safe. For example, some abused children booby trap their bedrooms in an effort to protect themselves. Compulsive behaviors may help them maintain a sense of control over panic, anxiety, and fear reactions. For example, being compulsively busy may keep an abused child from thinking about the abuse and experiencing fear reactions.

3. *Escape.* Many children resort to staying away from home and/or the abuser or running away to escape. They might also withdraw and isolate themselves from others in an effort to maintain a sense of safety. Addictions and compulsive behaviors are common escape mechanisms.

4. *Addictions and compulsions.* Addictions and compulsions of any sort (drugs, alcohol, money spending, sex, danger, chaos and cri-

sis, gambling, food, work, relationships, busyness or worka-holism, associating with questionable people or participating in risky activities) are common ways in which survivors attempt to escape the pain of sexual abuse. Although such behaviors offer temporary respite, most often they become problems in their own right.

5. *Delinquent or deviant activities or behaviors.* Sexually abused children may resort to lying and manipulation of others in order to cope. These activities may later extend into delinquent or deviant behaviors and life-styles, including criminal behavior such as violence and prostitution.

C. *Relational Coping Mechanisms.* Mechanisms in this category may overlap with psychological/cognitive and physical coping mechanisms.

1. *Other-directedness and codependence.* Sexually abused children are taught to respond to the desires of others, often at the expense of their own needs. They learn to ignore or minimize their own needs and emotions while feeling compelled to serve the needs of others. A codependent relational pattern frequently extends into adulthood and includes excessive caretaking or smothering, martyr behaviors, and excessive self-deprecation.

2. *Withdrawal and isolation from others.* Many survivors feel extremely mistrustful of and vulnerable to others as a result of having been damaged by the deliberate actions of another person; consequently, the survivor might avoid contact and intimacy with others in order to decrease his or her vulnerability and to control fear responses.

3. *Relational addictions and dependence on others.* Some survivors do just the opposite: they become overdependent on others and on being in a relationship. Adult relationship patterns may mirror those of childhood. Survivors are often at risk for revictimization because of the many negative relational patterns they learned during the abuse and in its aftermath.

4. *Repeating abuse or abusing others.* Some children and survivors reverse their sense of victimization and powerlessness by acting

out their anger and by abusing themselves or others. In this way, they become the powerful person who inflicts abuse on self or others.

IV. EXERCISE TWO: COPING WITH SEXUAL ABUSE/ INCEST AS A CHILD AND AS AN ADULT

A. Objectives:

1. To increase members' awareness of how they or someone they know coped as a child victim of sexual abuse and later as an adult.
2. To determine some of the positive and negative aspects of these coping mechanisms.
3. To determine what needs are or were being met by the coping skills and to brainstorm healthier ways to meet them.

B. Distribute the "Common Coping Strategies of the Sexually Abused Child" handout and ask participants to spend approximately 15 minutes thinking about and making notes in response to the question "How did I or someone I know cope as a child victim of sexual abuse and later as an adult survivor?"

C. Ask members to choose two discussion partners—with whom they have not yet worked, if possible—and discuss their responses to the above question for approximately 10 minutes.

D. Next, ask participants to spend about 15 minutes responding in writing to the question "What were the positive and negative aspects of these coping mechanisms?"

E. Have members discuss their responses to the question in their triad for approximately 10 minutes.

F. Ask participants to work alone for another 15 minutes responding in writing to the question "What needs are being met by these behaviors and what are some healthier ways to meet these needs?"

G. Again, ask members to discuss their responses to the above question in their triad for approximately 10 minutes.

H. Debriefing: In the remaining time, leaders engage members in sharing what they learned from this exercise with the large group.

BIBLIOGRAPHY

Bass, E., & Davis, L. (1988). *The courage to heal: A guide for women survivors of child sexual abuse.* New York: Harper & Row.

Blume, E. (1990). *Secret survivors: Uncovering incest and its aftereffects in women.* New York: John Wiley.

Courtois, C. (1988). *Healing the incest wound: Adult survivors in therapy.* New York: W. W. Norton.

Davis, L. (1990). *The courage to heal workbook: For women and men survivors of child sexual abuse.* New York: Harper & Row.

Poston, C., & Lison, K. (1989). *Reclaiming our lives: Hope for adult survivors of incest.* Boston: Little, Brown & Co.

HANDOUT 1

FEELINGS OF A SEXUALLY ABUSED CHILD

Imagine a child who is sexually abused repeatedly. List this child's feelings:

_____

_____

_____

_____

_____

_____

_____

_____

_____

_____

_____

_____

HANDOUT 2

COMMON FEELINGS OF THE SEXUALLY ABUSED CHILD

✔ Fear or terror
✔ Anxiety or nervousness
✔ Confusion and betrayal
✔ Embarrassment and humiliation
✔ Anger and rage
✔ Shame and a sense of personal badness
✔ Disgust
✔ Guilt
✔ Self-blame
✔ Powerlessness and helplessness
✔ Depression and hopelessness
✔ Grief and loss
✔ Pleasure (in some cases)
✔ Powerful and on par with adults
✔ Desirable and special
✔ Cheap and used
✔ Trapped
✔ Vulnerable
✔ Isolated
✔ Secretive and silenced
✔ Overwhelmed
✔ Vigilant and watchful
✔ Unimportant
✔ Unreal
✔ Other feelings suggested by group members . . .

HANDOUT 3

COMMON COPING STRATEGIES OF THE SEXUALLY ABUSED CHILD

Psychological/Cognitive Coping Mechanisms
- ✔ Inner wisdom/helper
- ✔ Denial and the distortion of self and personal reality
- ✔ Alteration of reality and dissociative reactions
- ✔ Other psychological adaptations

Physical Coping Mechanisms
- ✔ Personal negligence and self-harm
- ✔ Control of self and environment
- ✔ Escape
- ✔ Addictions and compulsions
- ✔ Delinquent or deviant behaviors

Relational Coping Mechanisms
- ✔ Other-directedness and codependence
- ✔ Withdrawal and isolation from others
- ✔ Relational addictions and dependence on others
- ✔ Repeating abuse by abusing self or others

HANDOUT 4

OTHER COPING MECHANISMS

No two survivors use exactly the same set of coping mechanisms. This list reflects many common ones.* (Of course, lots of other people use these as well in many other kinds of situations.) Circle the coping mechanisms that apply to you.

denial	abusing others	staying super-alert
rationalizing	forgetting	sleeping excessively
creating chaos	leaving your body	not sleeping
repeating abuse	staying in control	humor
fantasizing	gambling	dogmatic beliefs
perfectionism	minimizing	running away
self-mutilation	staying busy	suicide attempts
compulsive eating	alcoholism	drug addiction
compulsive exercising	anorexia/bulimia	compulsive sex
shoplifting	workaholism	avoiding sex
hiding behind a partner	gambling	spacing out
creating new personalities	taking care of others	avoiding intimacy

How I and Others I Know Coped

Question 1: How did I or someone I know cope as a child victim of sexual abuse and later as an adult?

_____

_____

_____

_____

_____

_____

Question 2: What were the positive *and* negative aspects of these coping mechanisms?

_____

_____

_____

_____

_____

_____

Question 3: What needs are met by these behaviors and what are some healthier ways to meet these needs?

_____

_____

_____

_____

_____

_____

*List is adapted with permission from Davis, L. (1990). *The courage to heal workbook: For women and men survivors of child sexual abuse.* New York: Harper & Row.

SESSION 6
ADULT SURVIVOR ISSUES: SELF-PERCEPTIONS

OBJECTIVES

✔ To increase participants' awareness of the negative self-perceptions resulting from sexual child abuse

✔ To increase participants' understanding of how these self-perceptions affect the adult survivor

✔ To help participants find ways to change these self-perceptions and mediate their negative impact

✔ To have participants discuss strategies for self-care and self-nurturing

I. OPENING THE SESSION

A. Review Sessions 4 and 5. Ask group members if they wish to comment on the content of these sessions and solicit their reactions.

B. Brief overview of Session 6.

II. EXERCISE ONE: NEGATIVE SELF-PERCEPTIONS OF THE SEXUALLY ABUSED CHILD AND ADULT SURVIVOR

A. Objective: To increase group members' awareness of the negative self-perceptions held by many sexually abused children and adult survivors.

B. Distribute the "Common Negative Self-Perceptions" handout. Ask members to make a list of negative self-perceptions and self-messages held by sexually abused children and adult survivors (themselves or someone they know). Inform participants that they are expanding on what they produced in exercises one and two in Session 4 and in exercise two in Session 5.

C. Ask members to share their responses with the large group. Leaders should list these responses on the flip chart.

D. Group participants are then asked to identify those perceptions and messages that come directly from the abuser. Leaders identify these by marking a star next to them.

E. Group participants are asked to brainstorm in the large group possible reasons for these negative perceptions and messages.

F. Leaders list these, too, on the flip chart.

III. MINI-LECTURE: THE DISTORTED SELF-IMAGE—NEGATIVE SELF-PERCEPTIONS OF THE SEXUALLY ABUSED CHILD AND THE ADULT SURVIVOR

Child abuse of any sort systematically damages the self-concept of the developing child. Instead of receiving the message that he or she is precious, unique, and in need of nurturing and protection, the abused child feels deserving of mistreatment and abuse and unworthy of special attention and consideration. Abuse often becomes synonymous with the child's self-perception. His or her needs are not important, but those of others—especially the adults in the family—are. The child learns that self-worth lies in the ability to meet the needs of others.

In Session 2, we learned about the characteristics of unhealthy families in which child abuse is likely to occur. To review, family problems often pass from generation to generation and from parent to child, thus negatively affecting the growing child. Some problems inherent in these families include addictions, chaos and unpredictability, and rigidity and arbitrariness, all of which can lead to different types of abuse, including physical, emotional, spiritual, and sexual. To varying degrees, all of these families have rules that they live by and that are taught to family members. Many of these rules are negative and disrespectful. Over time, these messages become embedded within the child's developing sense of self. It is the rare child who is not negatively affected by being treated with disregard and disrespect. Review the "Negative Rules and Messages in Troubled Families" handout from Session 2. Throughout the rest of this session, we will build on this information.

Of all forms of child abuse, sexual abuse has the potential for the most damage to the child, and of all forms of sexual abuse, incest is by far the most damaging. In Session 3, we identified aspects of sexual abuse/incest that cause traumatic reactions in the child victim and later in the adult survivor. These same aspects cause serious damage to the child's self-concept.

Sexual abuse/incest damages the child's sense of stability and security, which may already have been disrupted by other forms of abuse in the family and by negative family rules and messages. The sexual contact often begins in a mild form and may even be emotionally or physically pleasurable to the child. As it continues and intensifies and as the necessity for secrecy is conveyed, the child's perception of the activity may change. Pleasure or gratification frequently turns to fear, shame, and self-blame. Fear generates resentment, anger, and hatred. At first, these reactions may be directed toward the abuser, but over time the child usually turns these negative emotions back on him- or herself. Thus, anger and hatred become inwardly redirected.

If the child has disclosed the abuse without receiving help or if the abuse is evident to others and no one intervenes, the child's helplessness and negative self-view are reinforced. The child begins to believe that the abuse is deserved and that help or intervention is not deserved. The child may believe that potential helpers are so disgusted with the abuse and with the child that they deliberately refuse to help. Regardless whether this is the case, the child comes to believe some variation of this scenario.

As has been mentioned repeatedly in this workshop, the abused child distorts self and reality in order to cope. This distortion erodes self-respect and self-worth. The sexually abused child becomes alienated from him- or herself and often compensates by developing a false identity. Some adopt a rigid perfectionism to make up for what they believe to be their ingrained "badness." Others adopt a negative stance and lifestyle to flaunt their "badness."

Sexual abuse, especially incest, involves betrayal and negative influence by someone in a position of authority or who is important to the child. Emotional and verbal abuse of the child are also common correlates of sexual violation, particularly misrepresentation of the sexual activity and negative messages about the child's character. The child may be blackmailed by being told that the abuse is his or her fault and that he or she will be blamed, rejected, and despised for disclosing the abuse. These messages become incorporated into the child's sense of self.

Shame involves negative feelings about the self (as opposed to *guilt*, which involves negative feelings about behavior). Although shame is experienced by all humans at one time or another, it is intensified in unhealthy families and by abuse. Abused individuals are often said to be shame-bound. Shamed people attempt to hide that which is shameful to them. Secrecy often impedes victims and survivors from disclosing their abuse and being able to heal its aftereffects.

In summary, adult survivors commonly feel:
✔ Isolated, as if they were the only person who was ever abused
✔ Defective and worthless
✔ Shameful and bad
✔ Deserving of the abuse
✔ Undeserving of assistance and intervention
✔ Undeserving of care
✔ "Crazy" and unsure of personal perceptions and reality

✔ Helpless and out of control
✔ Powerless (or sometimes powerful if they had influence over abusive and/or powerless adults)
✔ Guilty

IV. EXERCISE TWO: CHANGING THE DISTORTED IMAGE— POSITIVE AFFIRMATIONS

A. Objective: To increase members' awareness of positive messages and affirmations to contradict and reverse the negative self-perceptions of the sexually abused child and adult survivor.

B. Distribute the "Positive Self-Perceptions" handout and ask group members to brainstorm positive self-perceptions and messages in an effort to separate self-esteem from the abuse experience (for themselves or someone whom they know). Instruct participants to review the "Negative Self-Perceptions" handout from exercise one and to develop positive self-perceptions that contradict negative ones.

C. Group members then discuss their reflections in the large group. Items are listed on the flip chart or chalkboard.

D. Group leaders should incorporate the items listed into the following mini-lecture.

V. MINI-LECTURE: CHANGING THE DISTORTED MESSAGE— AFFIRMATIONS, BOUNDARIES, SELF-CARE, AND SELF-NURTURING

Child victims and adult survivors need positive messages and reinforcement to contradict the negative messages they have received. Feelings of shame and self-blame often block awareness of the circumstances of the abuse or the context within which their negative self-perceptions were generated. The equation that what was done to the child equals the child's self-worth must be broken. Learning about abuse and examining self-perceptions and feelings such as shame and self-blame help initiate this process. Because negative self-perceptions become ingrained, they can be changed only through awareness and effort on the part of the victim/survivor to understand the circumstances of the abuse.

Charles Whitfield, an expert on dysfunctional families, states that abused individuals must seek out their true selves (the inner child). To do this, they must move from self-hatred and contempt to caring for and understanding themselves as children and later as adults. Whitfield offers the following steps in learning to love oneself:

Some Steps in Loving Myself
✔ Stop all self-criticism
✔ Stop scaring myself with fear thoughts
✔ Be gentle, kind, and patient with myself
✔ Stop needing to be perfect
✔ Support myself
✔ Ask for help with a safe support system
✔ Love my "negatives" (mistakes, shadow [or less than positive aspects of self], painful feelings, etc.)
✔ Care for my body (right nutrition, exercise, etc.)
✔ Mirror work (looking in the mirror to affirm and appreciate rather than depreciate self)
✔ Accept the things I cannot change
✔ Change the things I can
✔ Begin loving myself right now, unconditionally

Adopting these steps gives the victim/survivor tools with which to develop alternative—and hopefully more positive—views of the self.

Affirmations are positive statements that boost self-esteem and reinforce positive self-perceptions. Abused children and adults may initially have difficulty with affirmations because affirmations dramatically contradict ingrained negative self-perceptions. A survivor may feel that a compliment or an affirmation from someone "does not compute" with his or her feelings of shame, badness, and unworthiness. Survivors may benefit from simple *self-affirmations* such as "I am a good person," "I am lovable," "I am worthy of respect," "I have the right to say no," and so forth. Over time, these statements become internalized to form a positive self-perception on which to build healthy choices and behavior. These, in turn, reinforce positive self-perceptions, which then reinforce positive choices.

Visualization is a variation on verbal affirmations. For individuals who are more visually than verbally oriented, visualization might be more effective. With this technique, survivors visualize what they want (for example, learning to say no to a specific person, having fun, being in a healthy relationship) and work toward achieving what they imagine.

Self-definition and *self-protection* (both physical and psychological) are developed by learning to listen to feelings and establish boundaries consistent with inner responses. Abuse and negative family rules violate the child's physical and emotional space and inhibit achieving personal control. Individuals can learn to protect themselves by setting limits and establishing boundaries and by making their own choices and decisions. This contradicts the old message that they must meet the needs of others to ensure that others will not reject them.

Unfortunately, many survivors do not know how to establish and maintain boundaries, especially when it comes to saying "no" or choosing a course of action contrary to the desires of someone else. Learning to set boundaries takes practice, but it is possible. Setting boundaries enhances self-respect and enables the survivor to maintain positive power and control. (Boundaries and limits are discussed further in Session 7.)

Another way to emphasize self-worth and to build self-respect is to behave in self-caring ways and to self-nurture. As mentioned earlier, victims and survivors tend to feel alienated from themselves, their bodies, and their experience. Many survivors express their alienation and self-hatred by abusing their bodies, the locus of their childhood abuse.

Self-care and self-nurturing involve a wide variety of activities to care for physical, emotional, social, and spiritual needs and to cope with traumatic stress reactions.

✔ *Physical needs.* Self-care begins with body awareness and self-ownership. Meeting physical needs communicates and reinforces self-care and nurturing to contradict self-contempt and neglect.

✔ *Safety and security.* Refers to adequate shelter and freedom from unnecessarily risky behaviors, environments, or relationships.

✔ *Health care and physical maintenance.* Awareness of and responsibility for physical health; attention to adequate hygiene, sleep, clothing, exercise, nutrition, etc.

✔ *Stress management.* Attention to pacing oneself and management of stress. The emphasis is on maintaining a balance between too little and too much stimulation/stress. Relaxation is balanced with stimulation.

✔ *Emotional needs.* Awareness of self as a unique individual with a variety of emotional reactions and needs is essential to self-care. Adult survivors must deal with having been conditioned to selflessness and self-sacrifice. Awareness of physical reactions to abuse can lead to awareness of emotions and vice versa. Patterns of selflessness are reversed by paying attention to personal needs, desires, and reactions, then acting in accordance with them. Accepting compliments or the regard of others without automatically dismissing them may be a first step.

✔ *Intellectual challenge and stimulation.* Involvement in pursuits and activities that keep boredom and stagnation at bay.

✔ *Social/relational needs.* Involves the development of a range of interpersonal relationships, from acquaintances to friendships. (These are discussed in Session 7.)

✔ *Spiritual needs.* Attention to one's essence as a unique person and in relation to a higher power. Spirituality involves awareness of the *true self/inner child* as opposed to the *false self/damaged child*, and makes each individual responsible for developing self-knowledge, being responsible, and living authentically. It also means learning positive self-control and accepting what can or cannot be changed, then taking action accordingly.

VI. EXERCISE THREE: AFFIRMATIONS, BOUNDARIES, SELF-CARE, AND SELF-NURTURING

A. Objective: To increase members' awareness of strategies for self-care and self-nurturance.

B. Ask members to pair up and to brainstorm responses to the "Strategies for Change" handout.

C. Dyads then discuss responses in the large group, and leaders list these responses on the flip chart. Leaders emphasize how adult survivors have the power to take positive control of their lives to repair the damage to their self-esteem caused by sexual abuse/incest.

BIBLIOGRAPHY

Courtois, C. (1988). *Healing the incest wound: Adult survivors in therapy.* New York: W. W. Norton.

Ratner, E. (1990). *The other side of the family: A book for recovery from abuse, incest and neglect.* Deerfield Beach, FL: Health Communications.

Whitfield, C. (1989). *A gift to myself: A personal workbook and guide to healing my child within.* Deerfield Beach, FL: Health Communications.

HANDOUT 1

COMMON NEGATIVE SELF-PERCEPTIONS

List common negative self-perceptions held by sexually abused children
and adult survivors (you or someone whom you know).

_____

_____

_____

_____

_____

_____

_____

_____

_____

_____

_____

_____

_____

_____

_____

_____

_____

_____

_____

_____

_____

_____

_____

_____

_____

_____

_____

_____

_____

_____

_____

HANDOUT 2

POSITIVE SELF-PERCEPTIONS

List positive self-perceptions and messages that counteract or contradict the negative ones listed in exercise one.

_____

_____

_____

_____

_____

_____

_____

_____

_____

_____

_____

_____

_____

_____

_____

_____

_____

_____

_____

_____

_____

_____

_____

_____

_____

_____

_____

_____

_____

_____

_____

Handout 3

Strategies for Change

List some strategies for change involving self-care in the following categories. Be as specific as possible within each category.

Physical:

_____

_____

_____

_____

_____

_____

Safety and security:

_____

_____

_____

_____

_____

_____

Health care and physical maintenance:

_____

_____

_____

_____

_____

_____

Stress management:

_____

_____

_____

_____

_____

_____

_____

Emotional nurturance:

_____

_____

_____

_____

_____

_____

Intellectual stimulation:

_____

_____

_____

_____

_____

_____

Social and relational needs:

_____

_____

_____

_____

_____

_____

Spiritual needs:

_____

_____

_____

_____

_____

_____

SESSION 7
ADULT SURVIVOR ISSUES: LEARNED ROLES AND RELATIONS WITH OTHERS

OBJECTIVES

✔ To define the roles children play in dysfunctional, abusive families

✔ To increase participants' understanding of how these family roles affect their relations with others

✔ To help participants find ways to change problematic relationships

✔ To help participants discover alternative roles in their interactions with family and others

I. OPENING THE SESSION

A. Review Session 6. Ask participants if they wish to comment on the content of the previous week's session and solicit their reactions to it.

B. Brief overview of Session 7.

II. MINI-LECTURE: FAMILY ROLES AND THEIR EFFECT ON THE SEXUALLY ABUSED CHILD AND THE ADULT SURVIVOR

A role can be described as the way a person behaves according to his or her position in a system, a family being a type of system. A teacher has a specific role in a school; a doctor or a nurse has a particular role in a hospital or other medical setting. Roles lead to expectations on the part of others. The individual is expected to meet these expectations and to behave according to his or her role.

In all families, members assume roles that are understood by all family members, whether they are identified explicitly or not. Once a family member is established in a role, that role may solidify. Family roles often interact, complement, and reinforce one another. Changing one role is difficult because doing so causes others to change as well. The change of one family role may cause the whole family system to reconfigure.

Certain roles are common to unhealthy families, including those that are incestuous and/or alcoholic. In this session, five different roles will be discussed. (Refer to Session 2 for other characteristics of dysfunctional families and the context within which these roles develop.)

A. *Parentified Child/Caretaker/Hero*
    One of the most common roles in a dysfunctional family is the paren-tified child, also known as the caretaker or hero role. A parentified child assumes parental responsibilities at a very young age. This child functions as the adult in the family, taking care of the parents and the other children, and may also be labeled the *hurried, worried child.* This child is overresponsible and is expected to take care of others, regardless of his or her own needs. Other family members rely on him or her in ways that are mutually unhealthy. This child might also play the role of the *organizer* or the *accomplished one*, becoming very skilled at planning, even manipulating others, to get things accom-plished. He or she may function in a leadership role at school, in the community, and at home. These individuals are often independent and self-sufficient, capable of a wide range of achievements. It must be remembered, however, that their self-sufficiency and accomplish-ments are survivor skills that arise not out of choice, but because no one is available to care for them and meet their needs.

B. *Placater/Rescuer*
    Another role is that of placater/rescuer. This child takes care of oth-ers' emotional needs by "rescuing" them and by constantly making adjustments within the family or outside environment. The placater is expected to allay the emotions of parents and siblings by smoothing things out and offering reassurance. This child is typically very warm

and sensitive and may function as the emotional barometer in the family. He or she may possess enormous capacity to help others cope with their feelings and problems without any expectation of empathy in return. This role also exacts a price in that the child may not learn how to accept help from others and may be continuously anxious whenever conflict or discord arises. The child is likely to continue the placating role into adulthood when faced with stressful or anxiety-provoking circumstances.

C. *Adaptor/Lost Child/Mascot*
The adaptor or lost child learns not to ask questions, challenge, or respond to what is going on in the family. Basically, this child learns to survive by remaining unaware. Adaptors don't try to change, prevent, or deter any situation; rather, they "go with the flow" and do not assert personal opinions or control. They remain detached from their feelings and from involvement with others—hence the titles *lost child, forgotten one,* or *mascot.* They keep to themselves and are largely reactive. They adapt to the needs and wishes of others. As a result, their individuality is relatively undeveloped.

D. *Scapegoat/Victim/Martyr*
The scapegoat takes the blame for everything that goes wrong in the family. When a family is dysfunctional, family members know something is wrong. The scapegoat becomes responsible for the problem, even when it is totally outside his or her control. Scapegoating allows other family members to avoid looking at their behavior or to assume responsibility for family problems. By projecting problems onto the scapegoat, they avoid responsibility for their own behavior.

E. *Acting-Out Child/Class Clown/Delinquent*
The acting-out child specializes in disruptive or antisocial behaviors. These behaviors may have been learned at an early age as a way for the child to communicate his or her feelings directly or in a coded fashion. Disruptive behavior (or acting out) generates negative attention—which for some children is better than no attention—and also serves to communicate, albeit in a negative way. Class clowns

deflect attention away from a negative situation through behaviors designed to elicit positive reactions from others. Disruptive and anti-social behavior obscure the real problems—abuse or other negative family interactions.

F. *Other Roles*

Other roles and family patterns are also common to the sexually abusive family. As discussed in earlier sessions, such families deny their problems and present a front of normalcy to the outside world.

The roles of other family members may vary considerably but usually include variations of the following configurations. In the *ineffective mother/dominant father* configuration, the mother is helpless and passive, may be alienated from her child, and may resent the child for any favoritism shown by the father. This mother is often psycho-logically as well as economically dependent on her dominant part-ner. As a result, she may ignore blatant signs of abuse and even side with her spouse against the child out of fear of losing economic and psychological support.

At the other extreme is the *dominant mother/ineffective father*. The mother plays the role of dominant spouse who takes care of her ineffective partner. She eventually tires of this responsibility, causing the father to turn to a favored child (usually the oldest daughter) for the nurturance he no longer receives from his wife. Acting out sexu-ally with his child allows him to feel powerful and to obtain revenge against the woman he perceives as an unavailable spouse. The mother, in turn, may rely on the daughter for assistance in nurturing or placating the demands of the father.

The *overvalued son* is another common role in the sexually abusive family. The overvalued son may be coddled at the expense of the other children, especially daughters. He may be babied and dis-couraged from taking responsibility for himself and may be treated as quite special at the expense of others. Because of this coddling and overvaluation, this child exerts a great deal of power in the family. His siblings may be expected to take care of him. He may even sexually abuse his siblings, especially sisters. His father may serve as a sexually abusive role model; as a male child, he may capitalize on family rules that allow males power over females.

Family roles are resistant to change. In fact, adults often extend the roles they learned in their families of origin into their intimate relationships and into the next generation with their own children. Being stuck in learned roles often impedes adult survivors from relating to others in healthy ways. For example, the survivor may feel comfortable only in roles in which he or she is taken advantage of or in roles in which he or she takes care of others. Low self-esteem often contributes to the inability to change.

III. EXERCISE ONE: ROLES IN YOUR FAMILY

A. Objective: To increase members' awareness of the different roles of their family members.

B. Distribute the "Family Roles" handout. Ask group members to think about their own families and to indicate on the sheet whether family members played any of the roles listed.

C. Gather group members to discuss their responses in the large group. In particular, ask them to consider whether they were surprised by any of the roles that they identified as applicable to their family members.

D. Group leaders should tie this discussion to the discussion in the following exercise.

IV. EXERCISE TWO: EFFECTS OF CHILDHOOD ROLES IN CHILDHOOD AND IN ADULTHOOD

A. Objective: To increase group members' awareness of the effects of the five childhood roles in abusive families in childhood and later in adulthood.

B. Distribute the "Positives and Negatives Associated with Family Roles" handout. Ask group members to discuss the five childhood roles. How might a child be affected by these roles in childhood and later in adulthood, in negative as well as positive ways?

C. Ask participants to complete the handout by listing positives and negatives associated with each of the five roles. Engage the large group in a discussion, listing positives and negatives on the flip chart.

D. Group leaders should attempt to connect this discussion to ideas generated from the material in exercise one.

V. MINI-LECTURE: THE IMPACT OF ROLES, SELF-ESTEEM, AND ABUSE ON RELATIONSHIPS

The roles and rules learned in abusive families negatively affect members' ability to relate to others. In addition, the low self-esteem held by many abuse survivors make it difficult for them to establish caring, supportive, mature relationships. Adult survivors may play and replay the roles that they learned in their family of origin. Their interactions with others may be based on the roles learned in their families and reinforced by repeated abuse. How do these roles show up in adult relationships?

A. *The parentified child/caretaker/hero* might grow up feeling a need to be very self-sufficient and overly controlling of and responsible for others. This individual may lack emotional support from others and therefore be quite needy beneath the mask of self-sufficiency. This individual often relates to others by taking care of them. Although this person does not expect the support of others, he or she is very much in need of nurturance and support.

B. *The placater/rescuer* typically assumes responsibility for other people's behavior and is especially skilled at smoothing over conflict or discord. The placater/rescuer attempts to "calm the waters" in his or her adult relationships by trying to find compromise solutions even at great personal expense. Relationships that involve self-assertion or direct negotiation of conflict often prove emotionally straining for adults who have learned this role in childhood.

C. The *adaptor/lost child/mascot* is likely to become invisible in adult relationships. These individuals find it difficult to become personally engaged in adult relationships, exhibit few preferences and little self-knowledge, and virtually "go along for the ride." They let others set the agenda and assume responsibility. The adaptor assumes a childlike posture and does what he or she is told, thereby avoiding mature relationships and personal responsibility.

D. The *scapegoat/victim/martyr* takes responsibility and blame for everyone else's problems. These adults are used to being blamed. In adulthood, scapegoats may unwittingly seek out partners who revictimize them in one way or another or who allow or support their role as martyrs.

E. The *acting-out child/class clown/delinquent* continues to act irresponsibly and to feel angry. Persons who play variants of this role consider negative attention better than no attention at all. Thus, these individuals seek attention by entertaining others, engaging in dangerous and sometimes criminal behavior.

F. The consequence of these roles is that the victimized child and later the adult survivor has no idea how to establish relationships that are equitable and safe. Adult relationships may directly reflect the relationships and roles of childhood and thus keep the adult child "stuck in time."

VI. EXERCISE THREE: EXAMINING CURRENT RELATIONSHIPS

A. In the final exercise of this session, participants are asked to think about how their current relationships might be similar to or replicate relationships from the past. Leaders should emphasize that it is possible to change current relationships after past patterns are identified.

B. Objective: To increase group members' awareness of current relationships and their possible ties to family roles from the past.

C. Ask members to break up into dyads and to respond individually to the items on the handout "Past Roles and Current Relationships," then discuss their responses with each other.

D. Ask pairs to discuss their responses in the large group. Leaders should list responses on the flip chart and engage the large group in discussion. Emphasize how family roles in adulthood mirror past roles, how these past roles affect relationships, and how it is possible to identify these roles and to make changes.

BIBLIOGRAPHY

Courtois, C. (1988). *Healing the incest wound: Adult survivors in therapy.* New York: W. W. Norton.

Tainey, P. (1988). *Adult children of alcoholics.* Milwaukee, WI: Family Service America.

Whitfield, C. (1989). *A gift to myself: A personal workbook and guide to healing my child within.* Deerfield Beach, FL: Health Communications.

HANDOUT 1

FAMILY ROLES

The roles listed below are common in sexually abusive families. For each role, indicate whether someone in your family of origin (parents and siblings) or in your extended family (grandparents, uncles, aunts, cousins, etc.) assumed this role. You need not identify a person for every role listed, and it is possible for one person to fill more than one role.

Parentified child _____

Peacemaker _____

Dominant controller _____

Decision maker _____

Problem child _____

Confidant/helper _____

Good one _____

Provider _____

Scapegoat _____

Martyr _____

Indifferent one _____

Protected one _____

Baby _____

Enabler _____

Worrier _____

Lost child _____

Mascot _____

Rescuer _____

Placater _____

Adaptor _____

HANDOUT 2

POSITIVES AND NEGATIVES ASSOCIATED WITH FAMILY ROLES

The five roles discussed in the mini-lecture are listed below. How might individuals who assumed these childhood roles be affected either positively or negatively in childhood and later in adulthood?

1. *Parentified Child/Caretaker/Hero*

    Positives in childhood: _____
    _____
    _____

    Positives in adulthood: _____
    _____
    _____

    Negatives in childhood: _____
    _____
    _____

    Negatives in adulthood: _____
    _____
    _____

2. *Placater/Rescuer*

    Positives in childhood: _____
    _____
    _____

    Positives in adulthood: _____
    _____
    _____

Negatives in childhood: _____
_____
_____

Negatives in adulthood: _____
_____
_____

3. *Adaptor/Lost Child/Mascot*

   Positives in childhood: _____
   _____
   _____

   Positives in adulthood: _____
   _____
   _____

   Negatives in childhood: _____
   _____
   _____

   Negatives in adulthood: _____
   _____
   _____

4. *Scapegoat/Victim/Martyr*

   Positives in childhood: _____
   _____
   _____

   Positives in adulthood: _____
   _____
   _____

Negatives in childhood: _____

_____

_____

Negatives in adulthood: _____

_____

_____

5. *Acting-Out Child/Class Clown/Delinquent*

Positives in childhood: _____

_____

_____

Positives in adulthood: _____

_____

_____

Negatives in childhood: _____

_____

_____

Negatives in adulthood: _____

_____

_____

HANDOUT 3

PAST ROLES AND CURRENT RELATIONSHIPS

1. List three important current relationships in your life (with a family member, co-worker, school relationship, social relationship, etc.).

   _____

   _____

   _____

2. How do you act in these relationships? Is your behavior consistent with roles that you play or played in your family of origin? Is your behavior consistent with any other roles that you saw enacted in your family of origin?

   _____

   _____

   _____

3. What changes would you like to make in these patterns of relating?

   _____

   _____

   _____

4. What might you do differently to change some of these patterned roles and behaviors?

   _____

   _____

   _____

5. What reactions might you expect from others to any changes that you might make in your behavior?

   _____

   _____

   _____

6. How will you cope with others' reactions? List the positive and negative ways that you might cope.

Positive: _____

_____

Negative: _____

_____

SESSION 8
SUPPORTIVE PEOPLE, SUPPORT NETWORKS, AND OTHER RESOURCES FOR RECOVERY

OBJECTIVES

✔ To help participants determine safe and supportive people in their lives

✔ To introduce the concept of personal boundaries

✔ To increase participants' understanding of why a support network is useful and to generate strategies for developing one

✔ To increase participants' awareness of resources for support in their community, whether self-help or professional

✔ To close and evaluate the workshop

I. OPENING THE SESSION

A. Review Session 7. Ask members if they wish to comment on the previous week's session.

B. Brief overview of Session 8.

II. MINI-LECTURE: IDENTIFYING SUPPORTIVE PEOPLE

As discussed in an earlier session, child victims and adult survivors of sexual abuse often distrust other people, an understandable reaction in that their trust was exploited. Child victims first learn to mistrust other family members; this mistrust then extends outside the family to other people in the community.

The interpersonal styles of adult survivors vary greatly. Some are loners who do not develop close relationships with others or allow anyone to get close to them. Although most survivors develop relationships with others, they often maintain a facade of sociability and connection while remaining mistrustful and isolated. Some survivors develop relationships of some depth, but still have misgivings about trust and possible betrayal. Still other survivors are fortunate to have had someone who cared and who helped them learn needed skills to develop secure and stable attachments in childhood, adolescence, or adulthood.

As has been emphasized throughout this workshop, many formerly abused adults do not disclose what happened to them as children and thus lack the support and understanding that they so critically need to initiate the healing process. It is hoped that this workshop will assist participants to learn ways to change negative self-perceptions and to engage in new roles and positive relationships with others. According to Ellen Ratner in *The Other Side of the Family*,

> *Resolving the trauma of abuse, incest, and neglect requires reaching out, opening up, and sharing with others. It means taking a risk for growth, making friends, and building a support system. Even though the recovery process can feel frightening at times—and may leave you feeling vulnerable and exposed—do not hold back from reaching out to others. No one can heal the scars of abuse alone.[1]*

Developing a support network is a crucial task in recovering from abuse. It is essential that survivors develop relationships slowly, testing relationships to determine whether they are supportive and safe (trustworthy) as opposed to unsupportive and unsafe (untrustworthy). The following brainstorming exercise is designed to help you determine the characteristics of individuals who are safe and supportive versus those who are unsafe and unsupportive.

III.   EXERCISE ONE: SAFE/TRUSTWORTHY VERSUS UNSAFE/UNTRUSTWORTHY PEOPLE

A. Objectives:

1. To increase group members' ability to distinguish between safe and unsafe people.
2. To help members realize that they already recognize many of the characteristics of safe versus unsafe people, although they may not have been taught to apply this knowledge in relationships.

B. Distribute the "Characteristics of Safe versus Unsafe People" handout. Ask members to break into triads to brainstorm and list on the handout characteristics of safe and unsafe people. The whole group then engages in a discussion of the identified characteristics. On the flip chart, leaders list characteristics of safe/trustworthy people on one side and characteristics of unsafe/untrustworthy people on the other side.

C. Following this discussion, the leaders distribute the "Questions to Ask before Allowing Yourself to Be Vulnerable to Another Person" handout for members to read and discuss. Leaders and members look for overlap between what was listed on the flip chart and information on the handout.

IV. MINI-LECTURE: VALUE OF A SUPPORT NETWORK

Now we expand our discussion of how to identify supportive people to how to develop a network of supportive people. Survivors need to develop a network gradually. They may wish to start with one person whom they find trustworthy and dependable and build from there. It is not good strategy to become overly dependent on one person or to consider one person to be the extent of a support system. Although this strategy is certainly understandable, it is not very useful. The supportive person may be drained by having to meet all of the relationship needs of the survivor. A network, in contrast, has more resources and flexibility. It consists of people with connections to various aspects of the adult survivor's life. Individuals in the network may have some ties among themselves or may be completely separate from one another. The common denominator for all members of the network is the individual who has developed the network.

Forming a network is a time-consuming process that should be under-taken slowly. It can take years! Building a support network means not only having friends but learning to be a friend. Mutual reliance is a key element. A network of supportive others does not mean that everyone in it is a perfect friend. Rather, it consists of a group of people who, by and large, are reliable and trustworthy and who provide a safety net, a cush-ion, and support during life's ups and downs.

It is important to have a reliable and fairly stable personal network. It can include individuals from various life spheres, such as work, neigh-borhood, school and college, church acquaintances, and recreational friends, in addition to members of self-help or support groups, therapy groups, and professional therapists or other helping professionals. Each of these relationships involves some give and take on the part of both parties in order to develop a base of mutual trust. The following is an example of a personal network:

✔ *Suzie*, an old college chum, with whom you can remember good times and bad. Through Suzie, you stay in contact with or learn about other acquaintances and friends from that period of your life. You and Suzie maintain active contact and see each other occasionally throughout the year.

✔ *Linda*, your best friend, with whom you communicate almost every day. You share gossip about mutual friends and acquain-tances, circumstances at work, other life events, and your family. Your relationship is largely built on trust and experience with each other. At times you tend to overrely on each other. She can be somewhat depressed and anxious. At those times you support her. She knows about your history of abuse and has been very responsive and supportive to you.

✔ *Joe*, your next-door neighbor, who is friendly and outgoing. You share news of the neighborhood and he watches out for your safety. You watch each other's homes and pets when either of you is away.

✔ *Gwen*, a co-worker with whom you share a lot and with whom you are able to "de-stress" from a hectic day's work. She confides in you and uses you as part of her support system. She is an adult child of an alcoholic and tends to overwork. She has been attending adult children of alcoholics meetings. She tells you about them and how she is learning to become more self-nurturing and to rely on more than one friend at a time. She, too, is learning to reach out.

✔ *Loren*, a friend from high school who lives across the country. You talk together on the telephone maybe four or five times a year, but when the going gets rough you know that you can contact Loren and obtain a sympathetic response. He has been available to visit or to take vacations with.

✔ *Lorraine*, another neighbor with whom you have slowly developed a relationship. You now can spend Friday nights together watching old movies and comparing notes about your respective cats. You house sit and pet sit for each other on a routine basis. Although you don't know Lorraine as well as you'd like, she is someone whom you think you can trust.

An effective personal network requires mutual responsibility and a lot of "give and take." For some adult survivors, a personal network actually replaces the family network, which may have never functioned for them and which continues to be unreliable. A personal network allows survivors to learn that not all people will hurt them and make unreasonable demands without giving anything in return—people exist who will provide support, empathy, and reassurance.

Of course, survivors must select their network members carefully, paying a lot of attention to trustworthiness and reliability. It is important for survivors to base their judgments on a person's actions, not only on his or her words. For example, if an acquaintance says she will do something for you and then doesn't follow through, a mixed message is conveyed. Such a discrepancy might be overlooked once or twice, but if it occurs regularly, it suggests that this person is not reliable and should not be trusted to follow through.

Survivors also need to understand that they have choices in their adult relationships. As children, they were vulnerable and powerless, with little or no freedom to choose. In adulthood, however, they have both the power and the right to choose the people with whom they wish to spend time and interact.

V. EXERCISE TWO: ASSESSING YOUR CURRENT SUPPORT NETWORK

A. Objective: To increase group members' awareness of their own friendship and support network.

B. Each member works alone, responding to the "Assessing Your Current Support Network" handout.

C. Group members then discuss in the large group what they have learned about themselves and their support network by virtue of completing the handout.

D. Group members break into dyads and work together on the "Developing a Support Network" handout.

E. Gather participants together and ask them to discuss what they learned from completing the handout. Leaders should emphasize that personal power and control are available to adults as they make relationship choices. The ability to choose was not available in childhood.

VI. MINI-LECTURE: PROFESSIONALS AND PEER SUPPORT GROUPS

Professionals and peers can also be supportive in group settings. However, survivors who require specific support for abuse-related concerns should determine whether prospective support-group leaders have experience with and understanding of abuse issues. Professionals or peer support groups without such experience often cannot provide either the services or the response needed by adult survivors.

A. *Professionals.* Although most professionals did not receive information about child sexual abuse and adult survivors in their academic training, many have educated themselves through reading and continuing education and thus are knowledgeable about survivors and their needs.

Adult survivors may engage with various professionals: *mental health* (psychiatrist, psychologist, counselor, social worker, child protective services worker); *spiritual* (spiritual director, pastoral counselor, priest, minister, rabbi, or lay religious workers); *medical* (physician, nurse, dentist, technician); and *criminal justice* (attorney, police). In seeking out professional services, survivors can determine the professional's interest and experience in working with sexual abuse issues. Professional helpers, too, must be assessed according to safe versus unsafe criteria. Additionally, survivors should monitor their personal reactions to the professionals whom they interview and should assess how professionals respond to various questions. Although survivors should not expect immediately to trust or feel comfortable with the professional, they can determine early whether the relationship appears to be sensitive and respectful. Trust will develop over time within the context of the relationship.

B. *Individual and Group Therapy.* Many adult survivors need formal therapy. Therapists should be selected with great care. The therapist's experience, credentials, training, and interest in survivor issues should be evaluated, as well as the survivor's "feel" for the therapist. Therapists must earn the trust of the survivor by behaving in safe, trustworthy ways, by being respectful and caring, and by being aware of how abuse affects survivors personally and in their relationships. Sexual contact between therapist and client is never therapeutic or ethical. It is always the therapist's responsibility to maintain professional boundaries.

Individual therapy is negotiated according to the needs of the survivor and the recommendation of the therapist. Therapy ranges from infrequent, of short duration, and mild (less likely) to more frequent (once a week or more often), of longer duration (a year or longer on average), and intense (more likely). Longer and more intense therapy is often necessary because of the pain associated with abuse and the defenses the survivor has used to cope over time. These defenses must be dismantled slowly and carefully so as not to overwhelm the survivor emotionally. In post-trauma therapy, survivors often feel worse before they feel better. Good therapists understand the process and offer support while "nudging" the survivor to face the pain. They also offer hope and reassurance throughout the process.

Survivors benefit from both individual and group therapy, usually in that order, and sometimes simultaneously. The following comments concerning the benefits of support groups pertain to therapy groups as well.

C. *Can the Group Experience Help Me?* Ellen Ratner states,

> *In a group experience, the process of receiving accurate feedback from other group members can paint pictures of participants that differ dramatically from the images they have long held about themselves. All group members can use the strength and objectivity of the support group to develop a true, comprehensive picture of self.[2]*

D. *Support Groups.*[3] The work of exploring past abuse and neglect is made easier and is generally more complete with an adequate support system. If you cannot afford to pay for professional therapeutic services, a support group is a good alternative. Many public service agencies offer groups for both men and women. If no such group is available in your community, you might develop one. The purposes of a support group are as follows:

1. Provide encouragement to all group members
2. Share useful information and resources
3. Provide a safe place to express feelings
4. Offer mutual assistance and encouragement
5. Prevent isolation
6. Reduce shame and guilt
7. Provide feedback and encourage self-understanding

E. *12-Step Groups.* Al-Anon, Adult Children of Alcoholics, Survivors of

Incest Anonymous, or any related 12-step program can be used as a support group. Attending an appropriate 12-step program can help adults with a history of childhood abuse, compulsions, addictions, or some combination of these. The 12-step approach, as pioneered by Alcoholics Anonymous, is helpful because it:

1. Helps participants get outside themselves and be less isolated
2. Curbs negative behaviors and thoughts
3. Helps participants share with others
4. Helps express and relieve guilt and shame

Twelve-step groups have specific formats and procedures designed to keep meetings orderly and safe. Although 12-step groups are technically leaderless, a member is designated to open and close the meeting and to initiate the topic to be discussed at a particular meeting.

F. *Incest/Child Sexual Abuse Groups without Leaders.* These kinds of groups are loosely structured and without professional leadership; their purpose is to allow participants to share their experiences, to process feelings, and to receive support. If no sexual abuse/incest survivor group is available in your community, you may wish to develop one.

If you decide to begin a support group, the following guidelines are offered for consideration. Leaderless groups need structure if they are to function well.

1. Choose a simple, easy-to-apply format. For example, the format might be topic-related, open discussion, or a combination. You may wish to follow a 12-step format.
2. Choose a "gatekeeper" or leader for each individual session. Rotate leadership so that everyone has both the opportunity and the responsibility to lead discussion. Sharing power avoids power imbalances or abuse.
3. Make sure the meeting starts and ends on time. Meetings that

begin and end promptly serve as a model for dealing with others and for maintaining order and boundaries.

4. Set guidelines for managing emotional situations and ventilating feelings. Leaderless groups need structure and guidelines for safe expression of feelings so that participants do not become over-whelmed.

5. Develop a written group contract to identify goals, objectives, and group process.

6. Consider inviting local therapists and spiritual leaders to talk on specific topics. Variety enhances the participation and involvement of most group members.

7. If participants wish, they can develop a telephone contact list for support outside the group. It is wise to omit last names on such a list.

8. Decide how many sessions the group will run, how many members can participate, and whether the group will be open-ended or have stable membership. Develop rules for entry and participation.

G. *Sponsors, Mentors, and Role Models.* Alcoholics Anonymous, the world's largest self-help program, recommends that everyone in recovery have a sponsor or mentor. Sponsors are people who have been in recovery for some time and have faced major life stress (often an addiction and its accompanying problems) and learned ways to handle problems and be responsible and in control.

Adult survivors of child sexual abuse, like other recovering people, benefit from support. They, too, may find that a sponsor or mentor is of great assistance to them.

To quote Ellen Ratner:

Sponsors should be chosen carefully, be trustworthy, and have no need to elevate, put down, or control the person sponsored. The sponsor/mentor/role model should be there for the sponsored—to call, visit, and share with. . . . A sponsor is not a therapist. A sponsor is a peer role model, someone who chooses to share his or her experience, strength, and hope.[4]

A sponsor should not be a sexual partner. The relationship should have one primary focus—to support the recovery of both individuals, especially the sponsoree. A sexual relationship creates what professionals call a "dual" relationship. For abuse survivors, dual relationships can create anxiety and fear rather than provide comfort and support.

Many sources of support, ranging from peers to professionals to personal networks to more formal networks, are available in group and individual formats to assist adult survivors in their healing journey. Survivors need to develop their networks over time and to be careful in choosing trustworthy, reliable, knowledgeable, and sensitive network members. Recovery can be greatly enhanced when others point the way and offer encouragement and wisdom gained from personal experience. It is hoped that this workshop has served as a source of support and as a model from which participants might develop supportive relationships. Members may wish to continue to meet as a support group for one another.

V.   CLOSING AND EVALUATION

A. Closing Discussion and Termination

1. Objective: To give participants an opportunity to review and share their experience in the group.
2. Leaders ask participants if they found it difficult to talk about certain topics.
3. Thank participants for participating.
4. Ask participants what they found most valuable and most helpful.
5. Distribute a list of names and phone numbers of members who wish to share this information. Specify that the group may serve as the foundation for or an addition to a personal support network.
6. Encourage members to continue to learn about child sexual abuse and its aftereffects and to continue their own personal recovery within other educational groups, therapy groups, self-help groups, and/or individual therapy.

7. Encourage self-care and self-affirmation to contradict the negative messages of abuse.

B. Evaluations: Distribute the "Evaluation" handout and ask members to complete it. The evaluation gives group members a chance to evaluate the content and the process of the group.

NOTES

1. E. Ratner (1990). *The other side of the family: A book for recovery from abuse, incest and neglect.* Deerfield Beach, FL: Health Communications, p. 30.

2. Ibid., pp. 38–39.

3. The material in this section is adapted from Ratner, *The other side of the family: A book for recovery from abuse, incest, and neglect.*

4. Ibid., p. 40.

BIBLIOGRAPHY

Bass, E., & Davis, L. (1988). *The courage to heal.* New York: Harper & Row.

Courtois, C. (1988). *Healing the incest wound: Adult survivors in therapy.* New York: W. W. Norton.

Davis, L. (1990). *The courage to heal workbook: For women and men survivors of child sexual abuse.* New York: Harper & Row.

Ratner, E. (1990). *The other side of the family: A book for recovery from abuse, incest and neglect.* Deerfield Beach, FL: Health Communications.

Whitfield, C. (1989). *A gift to myself: A personal workbook and guide to healing my child within.* Deerfield Beach, FL: Health Communications.

HANDOUT 1

CHARACTERISTICS OF SAFE VERSUS UNSAFE PEOPLE

List defining characteristics of safe (trustworthy) vs. unsafe (untrustworthy) people. How can you differentiate between the two? What makes them different?

Safe/Trustworthy

Unsafe/Untrustworthy

HANDOUT 2

QUESTIONS TO ASK BEFORE ALLOWING YOURSELF TO BE VULNERABLE TO ANOTHER PERSON

It is important to be around people who are trustworthy. The following is taken from the book *The Other Side of the Family: A Book for Recovery from Abuse, Incest, and Neglect* by Ellen Ratner. She suggests an assessment of the following in building a network of supportive people. "Explore and examine their characteristics, behaviors, attitudes, and values to learn if it is safe to risk being vulnerable with them. Before choosing to be vulnerable with another person, ask yourself the following questions" (p. 34).

Alcohol/Drugs
✔ How frequently does he/she use alcohol or drugs?
✔ Does he/she have an alcohol or drug problem now?
✔ Does he/she get drunk, stoned, or high on a regular basis or at inappropriate times?

Directness and Risk-taking without Hostility
✔ Will your friend tell you and others only what you want to hear (people pleasing), or take risks and tell you unpleasant truths as well?
✔ Will your friend give you feedback in a way that you can listen to it?

Jealousy
✔ Is your friend envious or resentful of your life?
✔ Can your friend discuss envy if it is an issue to work through?

Life and Friendship Patterns
✔ What is your friend's previous pattern in friendships? Long-term or rapid turnover?
✔ Are your friend's personal stories consistent? Does your friend's life match up with what you have been told about the past and what others have said?

Negativity
- ✔ Is your friend negative, fault-finding, or critical?
- ✔ Does your friend have a biting, hostile sense of humor? Can your friend make jokes that are not mean?
- ✔ Are there times when you feel your friend's comments are hostile or biting, but you overlook them anyway?
- ✔ Does your friend make a big point of talking about a belief in honesty? (People who make a point of discussing honesty or ethics may be covering up their own dishonest feelings.)
- ✔ How important is being truthful to you?

Openness
- ✔ Does your friend seem open to what you say? Can this person hear your problems and difficulties, or does your friend minimize what you have to say?
- ✔ Does your friend have the ability to listen?

Treatment of Others
- ✔ Does your friend make fun of others' problems or is your friend compassionate?
- ✔ Does your friend have a reputation for talking about confidences and intimacies of others?

If you excuse or overlook negative or unsupportive behaviors in your friends in the hope that they will change, you are overlooking a lot. Remember that people do not change without much hard work.

Most important, is your friend loyal, caring, and respectful of who you are? If so, it is probably safe to share some of your childhood feelings and experiences as you work through them.

Have you clarified your dependency/autonomy issues with your friend? Does your friend understand how difficult an issue this may be for you?

Maintaining your network (e.g., letting your friends know when you are feeling stressed, when you would like to call, or even when you might want to stay over for a weekend) is important for your sense of well-being and safety. Even though you may be married or living in an intimate relationship, it is important to maintain a solid network.

Adapted from Ratner, E. (1990). *The other side of the family: A book for recovery from abuse, incest, and neglect* (pp. 34–35). Deerfield Beach, FL: Health Communications.

HANDOUT 3

ASSESSING YOUR CURRENT SUPPORT NETWORK

What friends might you wish to include in your personal network?

_____

_____

Person	Type of friend/ characteristics	How often you see
_____	_____	_____
_____	_____	_____
_____	_____	_____
_____	_____	_____
_____	_____	_____

Who is in your network now?

_____

_____

_____

_____

What category would you place them in? _____

How long have you known them? _____

How do they contribute to meeting your needs for growth and support?

_____

_____

_____

_____

Can you count on them to continue meeting those needs? _____

Are you able to be there for them when they are in need of nurturing and support? _____

IDENTIFYING YOUR PERSONAL NETWORK

People who like me, like to have me around, care about my being there:

_____

_____

People who share my values and have similar life-styles:

_____

_____

People who support and respect me for the things I do well:

_____

_____

People with whom I can have fun:

_____

_____

People who have known me for a long time, like me, and provide a sense of my past:

_____

_____

People on whom I can count to be there when I'm in trouble; people who will support me when I need it:

_____

_____

People with whom I can share things, who will give me a hug, and who I know love me and care about me:

_____

_____

People I can talk to about ideas, world affairs, new interests:

_____

_____

REVIEWING YOUR NETWORK

Do you see areas where you need some additional support? _____

_____

Are any of your needs not being met? _____

_____

Are you counting on just a few people to fill all your needs? _____

_____

Are you spreading your support network so thinly that no one is able to know you very well? _____

_____

Adapted from Ratner, E. (1990). *The other side of the family: A book for recovery from abuse, incest, and neglect.* Deerfield Beach, FL: Health Communications.

Handout 4

Developing a Support Network

Make a list of the kinds of things that you can do or the people with whom you can connect in order to broaden the scope of your support network. You may list various people in your life to whom you'd like to get closer; next to their names, list some of the things you could do to generate more contact with them. Remember—be selective and choose carefully.

Person	Ways to connect with this person
_____	_____
_____	_____
_____	_____
_____	_____
_____	_____
_____	_____
_____	_____
_____	_____
_____	_____
_____	_____
_____	_____
_____	_____
_____	_____
_____	_____
_____	_____
_____	_____
_____	_____

HANDOUT 5

WORKSHOP EVALUATION

Listed below are subject areas that were covered during the eight sessions of this group. Please mark each of these with the following responses: 1—most helpful; 2—somewhat helpful; 3—least helpful.

_____ The continuum of family functioning from functional to dysfunctional

_____ Some characteristics of the healthy, functioning family

_____ Some characteristics of an unhealthy, dysfunctional family

_____ The most common negative rules and messages found in dysfunctional families

_____ Some characteristics of post-traumatic stress reactions

_____ Some factors related to the severity of traumatic stress reactions

_____ Protective factors that moderate or dilute stress reactions

_____ Common feelings of the sexually abused child

_____ Common coping strategies of the sexually abused child

_____ Initial effects of child sexual abuse

_____ Long-term effects of child sexual abuse

_____ Negative self-perceptions of the sexually abused child

_____ Positive self-perceptions of the sexually abused child

_____ Learned roles in dysfunctional families

_____ How these roles extend into other relationships

_____ Characteristics of safe versus unsafe people

_____ The value of a support network

Using the same responses, please indicate how helpful you found the following:

_____ Information provided by the leader(s)

_____ Meeting other people with common concerns

_____ Working in small groups

_____ Large group discussion of specific topics

_____ Handouts

Please indicate whether the following statements describe your experience of the group:

Yes   No

____ ____ There was a proper balance between lectures and discussion.

____ ____ Overall, I found the workshop helpful.

____ ____ There was a proper balance between group discussion and working in pairs or small groups.

____ ____ This workshop helped increase both my intellectual and emotional awareness as an adult survivor of child sexual abuse.

____ ____ This workshop made me aware of my options for recovery.

____ ____ I am interested in participating in a therapy group for adult survivors of sexual child abuse here at our agency.

Adapted from Tainey, P. (1988). *Adult Children of Alcoholics*. Milwaukee, WI: Family Service America.

ABOUT THE AUTHOR

CHRISTINE A. COURTOIS is a licensed psychologist in private practice in Washington, D.C., and Clinical Director, Center for Abuse Recovery & Empowerment, Psychiatric Institute of Washington, D.C. She received her doctorate in counseling psychology from the University of Maryland, College Park, and is the author of *Healing the Incest Wound: Adult Survivors in Treatment.* Dr. Courtois presents workshops and lectures widely throughout the United States on the treatment of adult survivors of childhood sexual abuse.